"Truly a no B.S. guide for attaining the top financial position in any company. Practical advice and insightful real life experiences are laid out fantastically in this easy to read and enjoyable book!"

— Jerry Raphael, CFO, Stack Overflow

"Finally. A practical guide to what's needed and tangible steps to take to prepare to become a CAO. I wish this book was available when I first started my career!! Must read for anyone who wishes to become a CAO"

— Brandt Kucharski, Chief Accounting Officer, GrubHub

"Controller's Code provides valuable insight and perspective on the skill set, mentality, and values to succeed in Controller and CFO roles. It can serve as a checklist when hiring a well-rounded finance and accounting team."

— Wendy Walker, VP of Finance, Controller, and Assistant Treasurer at San Jose Water Company

"Controller's Code offers a map for young finance and accounting professionals as they launch their careers. Giving guidance and sharing insight, it will help many avoid costly mistakes and help better prepare them to achieve their career aspirations."

— Jim Walker, VP, Corporate Controller at Druva

"Technology as it relates to accounting and finance can be intimidating.

Controller's Code helps break down in an easy-to-comprehend fashion the importance of having a robust tech stack that contributes to the protection, growth, and success of a business."

— Nick Larchenko, Managing Partner at FinAcco

FOREWORD

I don't think you know anything about being a controller as an auditor. You understand the technical accounting — the debits and the credits — but when you take your first job as a controller out of public accounting, you have no idea what you're getting yourself into and no idea how a company works.

The biggest eye-opening experience for me came when I went from public accounting to my first job as a controller at a startup. I learned the hard way what to do and what not to do. I had spent six years at a large public accounting firm, where I rose through the ranks, and spent a year as manager. Even though the training was great, I really didn't know much about the internal workings of an accounting shop at a company. A client I worked with had become CFO of a startup, and offered me the job of controller. Great, I thought, it will be a lot of money and I was all excited for the opportunity to learn the nuts and bolts.

Then I got there, and I had no idea what I was doing. Zero. I mean, I knew what a balance sheet was and I knew what the income statement was, but I had no idea how to get anything into those statements or the work that went into creating those statements.

If I'd had this book back then, it would have smoothed the way for me. This book would have been my Bible. It would have opened my eyes to the breadth of what a controller does, and it would have given me a framework to build a great career.

I first met Mike through the current Chief Revenue Officer at FloQast, Ken Sims. Ken was looking for a job, and asked me my opinion of the company since he wasn't familiar with close management software. So I talked to Mike, and loved what he was saying. He understands the problem at a core level, and unlike the 99 percent of people who wouldn't take it any further, he was using technology to simplify a process that was literally centuries old. At a lot of companies, it's still paper and pencil or Excel workbooks. Mike had the vision to see that he could solve this age-old dilemma through technology, and his background allowed him to be one with that technology.

As much as I would have benefited from Mike's book in my first role as a controller, I think we need it even more today on account of how the younger generations have been raised.

When I grew up in Dallas, if your team won a championship game, you got a trophy. But if you didn't win, you didn't get one. You had to go through the process to get there and earn that trophy. But, when my kids were growing up, they were given a trophy at the end of every season, regardless of whether they won or lost.

So now we have the participant trophy generation. The result is we don't have a lot of experienced individuals right now. People are looking for money and title, and not necessarily experience. We've got people that have gone through the ranks, but the learnings are not really where they need to be.

They might be 30 years old, but they don't really have the requisite experience to be a controller or assistant controller or even accounting manager.

That's why I teach the courses I do for CFOs. Most people don't have the broad range of experience they need to be a great CFO. Companies aren't investing in their people. So I take all my scar tissue, and all my knowledge and give it to them, so that they can learn from someone who's been where they want to go. But I can't reach everyone who needs it, which makes this book especially valuable today.

One of the classes I teach is a one day a semester class at Wharton in San Francisco, and they had me come in for a career day not too long ago. I met a senior manager at a big accounting firm and she was looking to jump to be a CFO. And I told her, "You don't know anything about anything." She was shocked at that, and asked me what I meant. So I said, "Let me ask you a number of questions. How do you open up a bank account? How do you reconcile property, plant and equipment, when people don't tell you they bought any equipment? How do you negotiate an office lease agreement? How much tenant improvements do you need? You know the technical parts of stock-based compensation, but if you were given a stock-option contract, how would you input it into a system? Also, what systems would you get?"

That's one piece of what you don't know. And the second piece of what you don't know is managing other people. When you work at a large accounting firm, you're working with really smart and overachieving people. They're really motivated, challenging and awesome people. But as a controller, you go into an environment that is completely different. Not everyone has the GO GO attitude, and nobody has a deadline mentality. Not everyone there has the capacity or motivation to ultimately be a controller or a CFO. They may be great as the accounts payable person or the payroll person — and you definitely need those great AP and payroll people — but the level of sophistication and tenacity is multiple steps down when you walk into a controller role from an accounting firm.

I was super frustrated at my first controller job. I couldn't believe that people didn't want to work more than eight hours a day to get to the next job or to the next rung on the ladder. That just wasn't their motivation, so that was really hard for me.

A book like this would have helped me build a bridge between the technical skills that are a given for being hired as a controller, and the other kinds of skills you need to learn to be a great controller.

It's not just former auditors that struggle. I talk to a lot of former investment bankers who fail when they take that first jump into a CFO role. Like auditors at large firms, investment bankers work with obviously top tier people, but they flounder in their first CFO role because they fail to realize that they're not going to be working with that same caliber of motivated people.

In my first controller role, I learned how to manage people from all kinds of backgrounds. I came to understand the processes that recorded the activities of the company in the books and records. Then I started thinking about how to simplify everything with systems. Finally, I learned what it took to prepare an accurate and timely balance sheet and income statement and how to manage cash flow.

These are all things that Mike learned when he made the move from a Big Four firm to industry and as he stepped into the leadership role of building a tech company. These are some of what he teaches to the readers of this book.

Mike is a true entrepreneur. He has great knowledge about the ins and outs of being a controller. He lived through the paper and pencil and Excel process of closing the books because he actually did it for years. He understands what needs to be done at a core level.

It's a special kind of person who has the kind of vision that Mike has. I've worked with a bunch of entrepreneurs. When I was CFO of Yelp, I worked with Jeremy Stoppleman who came up with the idea for that company, and now that's a billion dollar company. But I'm not that guy with the vision, like Mike and Jeremy. I can help you get there and I can help you scale your business. Developing that kind of vision is one of the things that Mike wants to encourage controllers to explore in this book.

Unlike the typical CFO, Mike is not risk averse. He took the risk to create a technology that can help every company that exists, if they're willing to learn a new skill set. Because he's not risk averse, that allows him to think outside of the box. We need people like him.

When I talk about the need for people like him who aren't afraid of risk, I'm not talking about taking the risk to play games with ethics. Controllers have a very important role to play in terms of highlighting risk and understanding risk.

The controller role is high integrity and high ethics, and I don't think that can be said enough times. It's really important for controllers to stand up for what's right and to push back. Don't do what you know is wrong.

The greatest role that my controller at Yelp played was that he would push back on me. He wouldn't let me cross into the gray area. He was willing to push back on me and say, "Let's not go down that path." He would tell me how we needed to do things. And that was fine because I'm not a super technical accountant, so it was incredibly valuable having someone with the ability to push back to show me what the right path was.

Now it's super easy to pull the wool over the auditors' eyes and make them chase rabbits and hide things since the auditors really don't know much, in my opinion. It's pretty easy to do that, not that I would, and not that I would suggest that anyone even consider that. But with technology these days, auditors are learning how to really interrogate the GL, so that's becoming less easy to do.

But companies still need controllers with high ethics and high integrity to make sure things are done correctly. The controller needs to be the gatekeeper. That's one bucket of what controllers need to do.

The other bucket of what controllers need to do is to provide the CFO with a lens to see around the corners of what's out there, and this is a big part of what Mike pushes controllers to embrace with this book. Typically what controllers have been doing is gathering information about the past. But by the time that information is presented, it's almost irrelevant.

If you can't see into the future and project that past information forward, you're almost not helpful. Given the advances in technology, you can get a computer or a lower-tiered person to produce the financials. Controllers need to be forward looking. They need to have a vision for the future of where the risks are, given where the business is going. They can't just focus on where the business has been.

Controllers today need to embrace technology and embrace new and different ways to get the numbers right. They need to embrace the future in terms of where things are going, and they need to try to look ahead. The great CFO looks around corners, and if they have a controller who can provide a lens and a road so they can see around those corners, that makes for an awesome working relationship.

Controllers and finance professionals who want to build that kind of awesome working relationship with CFOs and the other members of the executive team need to read *The Controller's Code.* This book will accelerate the lessons learned for those coming up through the accounting ranks. By passing on the knowledge from his journey, Mike will help countless people excel at their jobs. Maybe some will even decide that controllership isn't the right career for them.

If you want to be a great leader and a great controller, you will want to read this book. This is one way to fast forward your knowledge. You still need some experience, of course, but with Mike's book, you can learn from the trials and tribulations of one person. Here are the notes for the path that one person took, and here's how you can follow. The world needs more people with this knowledge.

Rob Krolik is a managing partner at Burst Capital, serves on the board of directors and audit chair of The RealReal and Sun Basket and is an Aspen Institute Finance Fellow.

50%
59%

CONTENTS

Introduction xvii

PART 1
FOUNDATIONAL ASSERTIONS

1. The Story of FloQast 3
2. A Framework for the Modern Controller 10

PART 2
THE PEOPLE PROBLEM

3. Why are People Such a Problem? 43
4. Culture is the Key 48
5. Making People Your Most Important Asset 57
6. Trust is the Glue that Builds Teams 97
7. Accountability Isn't Just Compliance 117

PART 3
TAMING RISK WITH TECH

8. Challenges with Risk 135
9. Implement All the Tech You Can 154
10. Fix your Processes 169
11. What's in Your Toolbox? 179
12. Knowledge Connects Everything 190

PART 4
ANTICIPATING THE FUTURE

13. Creating the Accounting Team of the Future 217

Conclusion 239

Acknowledgments 241
About the Author 243
Notes 245

To Mom for inspiring me and Alison for supporting me.

INTRODUCTION

WHY THIS BOOK

My introduction to accounting was walking into a hallway in the Lionsgate building where there were hundreds of file cabinets and shelves with rows and rows of binders. At that moment, I realized that accounting was a summary of the events that all of those documents represented. And with today's technology, we have a better way to tell those stories.

Just think, over the last 40 years, accounting has changed from a largely manual, paper and pencil occupation, to a high-tech operation. The green 10-column ledgers, which hadn't really changed much since Luca Pacioli first documented double-entry accounting in 1494, and a ten-key were the main tools my mom used. For centuries, accounting was just on paper. You spent all your time just getting the information together and adding it up, then transferring those numbers to another piece of paper.

Then, we got computers, and accounting was entering the transactions in a system as quickly and as accurately as possible. But today, thanks to cloud software, apps, AI, machine learning, and automation, accounting is no longer heavy duty data entry, manual processes, long hours, and late nights, with barely time to make sure we got the numbers right, let alone think about them.

Today's accountants not only have the ability and time to delve into the numbers for new insights, but they have time to have lives outside of debits and credits. Automation and cloud technologies mean that a single click of a button replaces hours — or days — of tedious, error-prone work.

Technology means we get to do the high-level work that reflects the education we needed for our jobs. We're no longer doing the kind of tedious, mind-numbing manual work that, seriously, you don't need a college degree to do. Maybe not even a high school diploma.

Accounting textbooks from just a few years before my time included helpful hints for finding errors in manually tabulated columns of numbers. Now, universities are scrambling to add coursework in data analytics and IT to their accounting programs, courses that didn't exist a few years ago.

Technology has changed the way we do everything. The

phone in your pocket has more power than the Apollo computers that sent a man to the moon, and those computers were the size of a car. We can ask our phones for restaurant suggestions in a new town, and they'll give us directions on how to get there. We use our phones for banking, news, email, engaging with friends on social media — almost everything but making phone calls.

BEAN COUNTERS NEED NOT APPLY

It used to be that the primary role of the controller revolved around maintaining strong internal controls, regulatory compliance, historical reporting, and getting a clean audit.

But now, that's table stakes. The role of the controller is changing. Controllers aren't just scorekeepers anymore. They're taking on more of what used to be the CFO's job. They have a strategic role in the company. At FloQast, we recently surveyed 306 accounting and finance professionals, including 202 financial controllers.[1] According to that survey, 95% of respondents said that the role of controller is increasingly important and strategic. Controllers are no longer just the number crunchers and report compilers, but 69% say controllers are best described primarily as risk managers.

The complexity and fast pace of today's world combined with access to a flood of data and technology tools means that strategic work is being pushed down. CFOs are moving out of the number-crunching and reporting beat to take on more of the work that used to be the responsibilities of the Chief Executive Officer, Chief Operating Officer, and Chief Information Officer. CFOs today are evolving to be the right-hand to the CEO. I've seen this change firsthand over the last ten years.

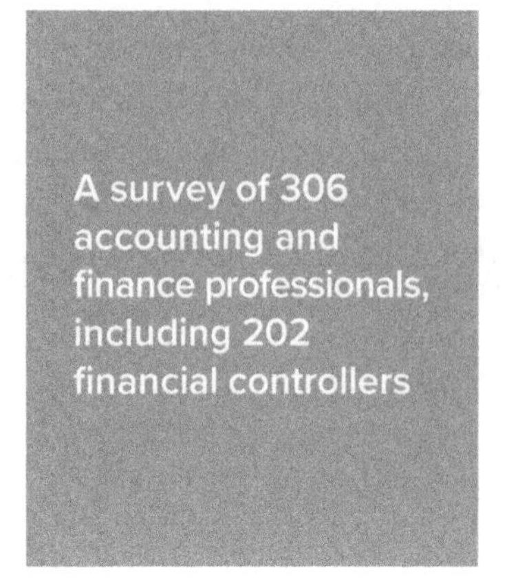

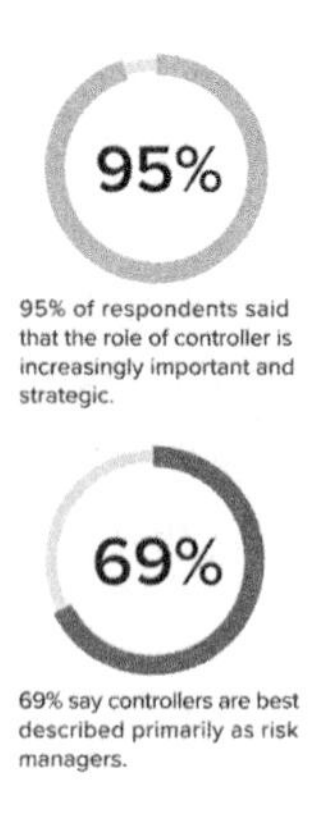

As CFOs take on more responsibility for the operations of companies, the COO role is being transformed, or even eliminated. Here at FloQast, Chris Sluty, a fellow CPA who's also one of the co-founders of the company, initially held that title, but as all of our roles have evolved, he's now our Chief Product Officer. As CPO, he's responsible for customer experience, which is an integral part of growth strategy for forward-thinking companies. We don't have a COO at all right now. And as the importance of technology explodes, CFOs and CIOs need to work closely together to ensure that the tech strategies of finance and of the business are aligned.

This means that controllers are taking on more of the C-suite responsibilities. Some are even being elevated to the CAO title — Chief Accounting Officer. So say good-bye to the old persona of controllers as bean counters, as the ones who say no to spending money, as the boring ones at the parties. Today's modern controllers have a more direct impact on the directions of their companies. They're no longer stuck in dark cubicles, siloed away from operations, but are collaborating with all parts of the business.

As Jerry Raphael, CFO at Stack Overflow put it:

> *The controller is uniquely positioned to influence the drumbeat of an entire organization. Once the financial close is completed, the controller should meet with senior leaders to go over the month's financial results. This monthly meeting is key to developing focus and alignment across the executive team for achieving shared financial goals. This in turn should result in the company moving faster towards achieving key business objectives.*
>
> *Senior leaders in every organization are tasked with building a predictable revenue and profitability machine. In today's business environment, controllers cannot merely process and compile financial results without communicating a clear and simple story as well. Supporting senior leaders with insights on results that are accurate and timely help form the basis for predictable outcomes.*

The career path from controller to CFO to CEO isn't a sure thing anymore. According to the 2018 Volatility Report by Crist Kolder Associates,[2] only 18.4% of sitting CFOs at the surveyed Fortune 500 and S&P 500 Index companies held the position of controller or Chief Accounting Officer immediately before their current position. This means if you've got your eyes on that CFO chair, you'll need to start taking on a more strategic role in your company.

You'll need to stop counting beans, and start planting beans.

As a controller, you control the data of your organization — and often not just financial data. Now it's becoming your responsibility to educate the rest of your organization about what this data means, and how that information can be leveraged to move your organization forward.

This change in the role of the controller has been happening for more than a decade. Back in 2008, Ernst & Young put out a report[3] based on a 2007 survey of controllers and finance executives at leading UK companies. In that study, 82% of controllers said their jobs had become more complex in the three previous years. According to one of the respondents, a finance director from a FTSE 100 firm, "The risk is that you never invest the time to work out what it is you need to do, and to identify what you are missing that would improve business operations. You need to look far enough in the future to remain ahead of the game."

Research by Deloitte and the IMA[4] identify a new class of controller, which they call "strategic controllers," who spend less than 60% of their time doing the traditional tasks of a controller. While traditional controllers, as identified in the survey, focus on learning about the new accounting standards and internal controls, these new strategic controllers look to improve their skills in "decision analysis, industry knowledge, statistical modeling/data analysis, and customer lifetime value." These new strategic controllers ask for a seat at the table — and are getting it.

Getting a seat at the table means you can't be spending your time doing the day-to-day work. You've got to build a team and develop systems and processes that give you the mental bandwidth to be available for those essential meetings. As Derek Mernagh, controller at Yelp, told me:

> *Once you have the day-to-day bread and butter in place, and you have the team in place to do that, then you can extract yourself out of the daily activities and be more strategic.*

Everything in the world is moving faster. As the authors of a report by Deloitte[5] said, "Finance teams need to understand that the world will continue to move even faster. We need to prepare ourselves to meet the demands of a business we haven't even seen yet."

Accountants aren't the only professionals whose work is changing these days. A 2015 book by father and son UK attorneys, Richard Susskind and Daniel Susskind, *The Future of the Professions*, describes the changes for professionals in the fields of law, accounting and finance, healthcare, religion, education, journalism, management consulting, and architecture.

In all of these professions, technology and the internet are democratizing access to the specialized practical knowledge and insights that used to be the sole province of professionals. It used to be that only the wealthy or biggest companies could afford the specialized knowledge that we can now access with just a few clicks of a mouse.

Today, services such as LegalZoom, WebMD, QuickBooks, and TurboTax provide online access to information and the services that we used to have to hire professionals for. Massive Open Online Courses, or MOOCs, made it possible for more people to enroll in classes at Harvard in a single year than have attended the university in person for its entire existence. All of these are disrupting the ways that professionals work. But as the Susskinds write, "We have found that many of the so-called 'disruptors' that we interviewed do not themselves regard their efforts as disruptive. They view them as liberating."[6]

For accountants in industry, these changes to technology mean that we have access to a flood of more accurate and timely information. Everyone from small business owners to Fortune 500 executives has easy access to relevant data, and often in real time. Accurate and timely data means they're making decisions based on actual data, not just pure instinct and gut feeling, which used to be the best information available.

GET COMFORTABLE WITH RISK, AND MAKE FRIENDS WITH TECH

A big challenge for accountants is that we've long been trained to be risk averse and tend to be slow to change. We're conditioned to avoid any mistakes. It's bad if we have to do restatements, or if we miss something big. And some errors can even land us in jail. So that fear of failure means we're reluctant to change.

Today's modern controllers can't avoid change. They need to embrace change, and take on the mantle of being a risk manager. Technology will play a big role in supporting that risk management. Rather than resisting tech, you need to be out looking for as much as you can get. You have the opportunity to participate in the technological transformation of your company.

Yes, implementing new technology can feel risky. But not implementing it can be riskier, especially if the competition invests in tech that propels them far ahead. According to a Forrester Research study cited in an article on CFO.com,[7] "businesses that operate on data-driven insight rather than instinct grow 30% a year on average."

Just think of big companies like Blockbuster, Circuit City, and Toys R Us that couldn't survive the digital transformation. The Sears catalog was the Amazon of the early to mid 20th century. Today, Sears is barely on life support, emerging from bankruptcy. Even Google may not be around forever, as implied by the title of George Gilder's 2018 book *Life After Google: The Fall of Big Data and the Rise of the Blockchain Economy*.

Technology needs to be your partner, or you'll spend all your time processing transactions, entering data, and tracking down mistakes in those error-prone manual processes. That's the reality I lived, when I was in charge of contracts at Cornerstone. I couldn't just be an A-student, with a 99.5% accuracy.

Get one contract wrong, and that could be a material misstatement.

We accountants need to be directly involved in the development of that technology. We don't need to learn to code, but we do need to learn to talk to IT and understand what's possible, and what makes business sense.

Over the last decade, controllers report spending significantly more time managing IT – IT that didn't exist just a few years ago. And with ERPs moving to the cloud, there's less need for a big IT department or resources. You don't need to know the details of how it all works but you do need to know how to use it. Let the digital natives on your team help the skeptics learn to use it and get comfortable with it.

Today's digital natives won't accept a job in your accounting department if you're not using technology that makes their lives easier. Lack of tech drives away talented young accountants who get frustrated when it's harder to get information from a legacy ERP than from their phones.

We're in the middle of a revolution in accounting and the way that businesses operate. Accounting and finance are moving away from being pure cost centers for businesses and into harnessing data to produce insights that create business value and bring actual dollars to the bottom line.

Finance leaders of the future need to become business partners. When we use technology to align the strategy of finance with the strategy of our organizations, we get to do the exciting work that moves our companies forward.

As Accenture reported in its 2015 report, "Finance 2020: Death by Digital:"[8]

> Finance is doing things that it never could before thanks to digital technologies. End-to-end multi-dimensional data

> access is enabling total visibility into both enterprise and customer data. The result? The finance organization will evolve from an expense control, spreadsheet-driven accounting and reporting center, into a predictive analytics powerhouse that creates business value.

By moving into this more tech-focused, strategic world where we're helping manage risk, we're helping with business processes, we're contributing more to strategic and operational thinking. There is a very real potential to grow beyond the "bean counter" stereotype.

IT'S NOT JUST TECH. IT'S PEOPLE TOO.

Rapidly changing technology isn't the only challenge controllers face. Controllers are pulled in way too many directions. They have to be proficient as technical accountants, but they also have to manage a team. And who will be on that team in the future might surprise you.

By the most extreme estimate, as much as 95% of the work currently done by accountants may be done by robots in the next two decades.[9] But, at the same time, a study by Korn Ferry[10] says that by 2030, there may be a global talent shortage of 85 million people.

For anyone in finance, that talent shortage is here, now. A recent survey of CFOs by Deloitte[11] puts finding talent at the top of their concerns, which isn't surprising.

Implementing technology will help with the talent shortage, but it also means accounting teams need the skills to use that technology. For some, it means changing the way they've worked for years, maybe decades. Instead of being a whiz with spreadsheets, which will still be one of our tools for a long time to come, controllers will need a team with new skills. Here are just a few:

- The ability to knit apps together to automate a process
- Analysis of soft and hard trends to understand the impact on the business
- Communication and presentation skills
- Strategic thinking

Today's younger accountants (and more than a few of the older ones) want a workplace where they feel like they're a part of something bigger than themselves. No one wants a job where they just go in and assemble spreadsheets no one will ever read. Nobody wants to feel immaterial. They want to help make the world a better place, too. They want a workplace culture that lets them be themselves. And if your company isn't providing that, just a few clicks on LinkedIn can get them a new position.

DON'T JUST AUTOMATE. INNOVATE.

Adding technology to automate your processes might not give you much bang for the buck if your processes are inefficient. Business process engineering has been around for decades. Way back in the early 1980s, Ford reduced their A/P department by 75% just by changing the way they processed payments to vendors.[12]

Instead of waiting for a vendor to send an invoice, matching that invoice to a purchase order and to what the vendor shipped, and then paying the vendor, which is how most A/P departments function, Ford's receiving clerks matched vendor shipments to purchase orders, and that triggered payment to the vendor. That change meant Ford trimmed the A/P head-count from 400 to 100.

Redesigning their process — and not implementing technology — saved the company considerable man-hours and dollars. Just imagine what your company could do by adding technology to processes that are already efficient.

Grafting automation on to an inefficient process is like making a Rube Goldberg contraption work faster. Change can be painful, especially when we're talking about disrupting processes that have been in place for years. And it might mean an investment of time you don't have. But if you can find a better way to get to the same place, it will pay off in the long run.

WHY I CREATED THIS BOOK

I created this guidebook to help Modern Controllers with practical, actionable steps to navigate these changes. One of the things that fascinates me is how difficult the controller job is because of all the different expectations. You're supposed to be a good leader, a good manager, a great reviewer, a great technical accountant, and someone who can speak in front of a CFO and presents fairly well. And now, you need to be an expert in tech as well.

But how do you learn to do all those pieces of your job? As you're moving up through the ranks, particularly the notion of leadership is not something that's really taught in accounting. Management is what's taught. Leadership isn't really brought up until you reach CFO level, if that's even part of your career trajectory.

While there are many books and gurus out there with guidance for accountants who work in public accounting firms, there are few models at present for finance teams in industry.

Most guides are how to do the various pieces of the work – SEC filings, loans, audit prep, IPO, etc. – but there are few sources of guidance, best practices, and examples for those who want to move into the future.

Throughout this book you will find stories from our clients and others who are moving forward to be Modern Controllers.

In **Part I**, I'll share my story about how my frustrations with the available technology and the highly manual processes that accountants in industry are stuck with led me to found FloQast. I'll also lay out the framework I'll use as a guide to success, which I lay out as equations (because accountants like equations).

- **Success = Culture + Technology**
- **Culture = People + Trust + Accountability**
- **Technology = Process + Tools + Knowledge**

Part 2 covers the challenges with people. The talent crunch in accounting isn't going to get better anytime soon. Solving the people problem means solving the Culture equation: Culture = People + Trust + Accountability. The culture at your organization and in the accounting department determines whether your team will be able to leverage the available resources — including technology — to create success.

Culture isn't just about having the right people in the right places (though that's probably the most important thing you need to get right). It's also about building trust that flows in both directions, so that those you work with trust you as much as you trust them. Accountability is what seals the deal: when everyone can see what everyone else is working on, and holds their feet to the fire to make sure it happens, then all your people can trust that their contributions will be honored.

Part 3 covers the challenges with risk. From our training as accountants, we learn to focus on the past. But today's complex world is forcing us to change our perspective and look to the future. I can't teach you how to build a crystal ball, but as co-founder of a tech company, I can tell you that embracing technology will help you get in front of risk and reduce it.

So in Part 3, I'll talk about how solving the Technology equation can help you reduce risk. Technology will give you the bandwidth to think about how to deal with risk. But just grafting the latest tech onto a bad process won't help, so you've got to clean up your processes as well. Combining those processes with the right tech tools not only gets you information you can trust, but it can also mean your organization can scale without adding headcount to the accounting department. Combining technology and processes lays the foundation for Knowledge. When you have the time to actually think, you can help your organization make the strategic moves that will keep it relevant.

Review Notes

Most of us started out as auditors, and when a reviewer found something that needed to be changed, we got review notes. Some reviewers were savage, and relished humiliating us and reminding us of the rank they held above us. Depending on your personality, that could either inspire you to work extra hard, or break your spirit.

But if we had a friendly reviewer, who was more interested in helping us learn to be better auditors than in making us feel badly about our mistakes, then that review note might include the reasoning behind doing something differently. Sometimes those friendly review notes were little nuggets of wisdom that could be used in different contexts, or acted as a gentle nudge to help us move to the next level in our careers.

In the spirit of a friendly reviewer, I've included **Review Notes** interspersed through the text. These are little nuggets of information that I hope will help you move ahead in your career. And since we accountants like to sign things off, you'll see my signoff at the end of every review note, so you can easily skip ahead if it's not relevant to you.

PART 1

FOUNDATIONAL ASSERTIONS

1 / THE STORY OF FLOQAST

As ever, the accountant in me saw the risk, the entrepreneur saw the possibility. So I split the difference and kept moving forward.
—Phil Knight

"Welcome aboard! Here's your desk and your computer. All the files you need are on the shared drive. Go figure out how we do stuff here."

That was pretty much the extent of my onboarding at

Cornerstone OnDemand, a pre-IPO startup, where I was hired to be a senior accountant after putting in a grueling 3½ years as an auditor in the LA office of Ernst & Young. At EY, I had been part of a team auditing entertainment companies including Lionsgate and Mark Burnett Productions (who worked with Survivor, Tyler Perry, and Twilight).

After getting my degree in accounting at Syracuse University, I had returned home to Los Angeles. Chris Sluty, my college roommate and co-conspirator on accounting class projects, stayed on the east coast, where he was from. I was glad to be back in a warm climate. Chris and I compared notes about life in big accounting firms.

I was a go-getter at EY and worked a ton of hours. By the time I decided to get out of public accounting, I had come in number one in the LA office with the most billable hours — 2,500. Putting in that many billable hours meant I had actually worked over 3,000 hours, putting in an average of 60 hours per week. By the end of my time at EY, I was burned out.

At Cornerstone, I was the fifth hire in the accounting department, and the company, which already had about 100 employees, was growing fast. We were gearing up for an IPO in the next 12 or 13 months. I had effectively no onboarding and I found myself painfully digging through our accounting system, which was not really existent at the time. We were transitioning from QuickBooks to NetSuite, so there was no single source of truth.

I was trying to learn how to use QuickBooks, but had little motivation since we were abandoning it soon. Instead, I worked on learning NetSuite and tried to help with the implementation. I was also learning about what accounting on the industry side was like. Even though I'd spent almost four years at a Big Four firm, my only previous experience with closing the books was in a college class where we had a manual bookkeeping project with maybe 20 transactions that we had to record on paper mockups of real accounting records.

I spent two weeks on my own digging through all the documentation we had around the accounting department to try to learn about Cornerstone and how things got done. I opened every folder to see what was in there and read random documents. "What's in here? Oh look, there's a policy about revenue. Interesting. Let me start digging through that." Or, "Here's a reconciliation for accounts receivable. Let me start learning about that."

Back at EY, we auditors had used an internally developed tool called Global Audit Methodology, or GAMx, for short. This software helped us organize, plan, and perform our audits. It helped us get our checklists in order. All of our processes were stored and documented in there, and work would get assigned to various team members. You could see who was the preparer and who was the reviewer of different tasks. We would save all our documents along with the workpapers. GAMx helped our managers track where we stood with the audit, and they could make sure all the documentation was saved in one nice, clean place.

So then the following year, it was very easy for us to refer back to what we did in the prior year. It would keep our files intact, wrapped up, and in one location for as long as we were required to keep the backup for our audits.

Exchanging notes with Chris, I learned that he was working with a similar tool at Rothstein Kass, an East coast mid-tier firm that later merged into KPMG.

GAMx kept everyone on the team accountable and on the same page. It helped with transparency and making sure that all of our procedures were performed, that all the i's were dotted and the t's were crossed.

Naively, I thought that accountants in industry would have something similar. But as I was learning from my intro to the private world, there was a serious lack of organization. At first, I chalked the mess up to start-up issues. But, as I soon discovered, it wasn't just a start-up issue. Hardly anybody in industry was using software to organize the month-end close. It was a mess.

Since we were gearing up for our IPO, we began closing the books on a regular cadence. We started quarterly with soft monthly closes. When we went public, we transitioned to doing hard monthly closes, which was much more difficult.

All along the way, we're closing the books and we're hiring more team members. The work was getting divvied up amongst the new people, and with that, it was really difficult to keep track of where things were being saved, who was working on what, and making sure that everything was actually getting done. Tasks were assigned and reassigned almost randomly, based on who had too much work on their plate. And there was no central way to keep track of who was doing what.

So, even though this was a SaaS company, the weird thing was that we did not use a ton of technology, especially in accounting. It was a strange contrast to EY, where we had an internal IT department that created tools for everyone to use. Instead of bringing on a tool like Zuora to help manage all the revenue from contracts, the leadership at Cornerstone just kept bringing on more Big Four CPAs.

I was the revenue guy, so I had to do the revenue for every contract. One day, I sat down and crunched the numbers, looking at the projections for how fast we were growing. By

Q3 I was going to be working 90 hours a week to keep up. So I asked the CFO what the plan was to help me out. They kind of waffled at first, and talked about bringing in some temps to help out. Then they gave me a totally inadequate budget to hire a CPA with two years of Big Four experience. At that point I quit.

Three months later, I did go back to them, but as an hourly consultant to do the revenue again. They made it worth my time because they'd had to hire three consultants to do my job. Cornerstone grew so much that by the time I left for the second time, 18 months later, we needed 11 to manage the five revenue accounts. This was a trial balance with 200 accounts, and 11 people out of a 50 person accounting team, just for revenue.

THERE HAS TO BE A BETTER WAY

But I kept thinking about the mess of the month-end close. "There has to be a better way," I thought. "If EY could build their own audit management tool, why can't I build something like that for corporate accounting departments?" Every audit firm has a tool to manage workflow. But private companies don't.

And the weird thing is that it's sort of typical for accountants to put in their two years in the Big Four, and then go to industry. So all these accountants are coming through the ranks, from an environment where they have an audit management tool to an environment where there isn't anything but chaos and stress. Where no one has anything even closely resembling standard procedures, and a lot of the time, the only checklists are in someone's head.

In 2013, I started looking into the startup community for help to build a tool. LA has a really vibrant startup community, which surprises a lot of people. Most everyone thinks that only happens in Silicon Valley. It was there that I met Cullen Zandstra, an awesome software engineer who'd spent a decade working on different projects. He had been involved with MySpace, and had grown to despise all the social apps. Photo sharing apps were "just not at all my jam," he told me.

After the superficiality of MySpace, he really liked the utilitarian, B2B, and "unsexy" prospect of building something to help accountants in businesses. He was excited about the prospect of dramatically changing an aspect of the lives of those accountants.

While I was still at Cornerstone, my good friend Chris Sluty came to LA. At first, he was only there on a four-month rotation with his current CPA firm. Chris moved in to our spare bedroom the week after my wife and I got married, and ended up staying with us for eight months. Chris and my wife had known each other since freshman year at Syracuse, so it wasn't like some random dude crashing on our couch. Chris liked LA so much that his four-month rotation turned into permanently moving to LA.

I started talking to Chris about my ideas, and showed him some of my prototypes. Then Chris decided he didn't want another busy season. So the audit partner he worked with got him a bunch of interviews, and on the same day that FloQast got into Amplify LA, Chris got a job offer. But I convinced him to come work with Cullen and me instead.

Our first office was a two-bedroom house, and we all did a little of everything, except coding, which was all Cullen. Cullen built a prototype, and Chris would go in the next day and try to break it.

FloQast was the first FloQast customer. I built the first checklist, and as soon as Chris came on board, I handed the month-end close off to him. Chris, who had never closed the books before for any company, just followed what I had done the month before, and got it done, no problem. A far cry from what I had experienced at Cornerstone.

Slowly, we started getting customers. And we asked them for feedback so we could make it better. By the end of our first year, 58 businesses were using FloQast, and we were hearing from controllers how this was changing their lives.

Fast forward to early 2020, and we've raised over $93 million from top tier venture firms, and we have 150 employees and more than 800 happy, happy customers.

2 / A FRAMEWORK FOR THE MODERN CONTROLLER

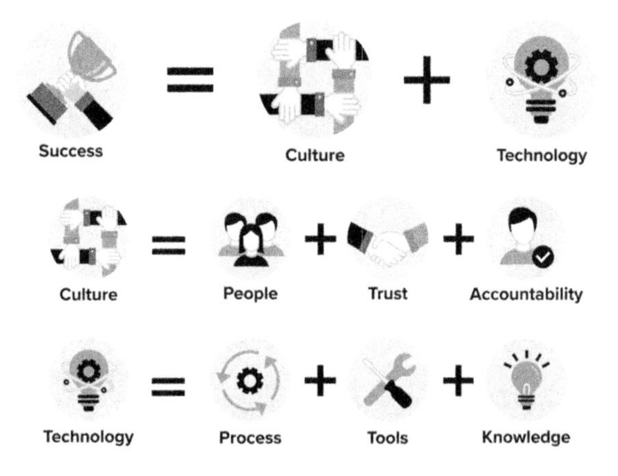

High achievement always takes place in the framework of high expectation.
—Charles Kettering

Just like FloQast gives controllers a framework for closing the books and tracking monthly tasks and projects, having a framework for thinking about your work will help you create a strategy out of chaos. Let me lay out this framework, and then I'll delve into the details of each part.

- **Success = Culture + Technology**
- **Culture = People + Trust + Accountability**
- **Technology = Process + Tools + Knowledge**

SUCCESS = CULTURE + TECHNOLOGY

When I say Success, I'm talking about all the levels of success: success in your career, success as a leader of a great accounting department, success in helping your company grow and develop, and success in helping your community.

How do we define success? …

Some controllers are content in their position. They like being in the controller's seat. For these controllers, attaining work-life balance while excelling in their jobs is the goal. They want to spend more time with their families and on pursuits outside the office, and they want to make a difference in their company as the controller.

How can they do this? Some of these modern controllers are taking on ownership of more and more non-financial data. They're leveraging technology that enables their accounting teams to become the data analysts that many small and midsize organizations don't have, but really need. They're helping their CFO, who is taking on more of a strategic role, by taking on some of the typical CFO responsibilities.

For other controllers, career advancement is the goal. These controllers may have their eye on the CFO (or even CEO) position. How can they make a difference in their current role running the accounting function that enables them to stand out in a crowded field?

In 2007, about a third of CFOs came from the controller role, according to a Korn Ferry survey.[1] That number seems to be dropping. The 2018 Crist Kolder Volatility Report[2] found that only 18.4% of current CFOs came from the controller position.

The CFO role itself is becoming more complex, and fewer controllers are seen as having the needed skills in leadership, strategic thinking, collaboration, communications, and operations that are needed to be successful as a CFO.

So controllers who want to move into the CFO seat need to do as much as they can to get out of the debits and credits. They have to invest in themselves and be willing to stretch their abilities. At the very least, meeting folks in the organization outside of finance and establishing relationships with them is essential. Putting in a tour of duty outside of finance to work in operations or IT or investor relations can give these future CFOs the broad business experience they need.

Regardless of which path you're on, success also means that because you have created the right culture, your people understand the **Why** that guides your organization. This idea comes from Simon Sinek's book, *Start with Why*. Sinek says that great leaders inspire people to act by clearly explaining the Why behind a company.

When your team clearly understands the **Why** of the company, and **Why** they're performing a task, it opens up possibilities to innovate and find a better way to do things. It sets the target that your people are aiming for. Giving your people the technology they need to execute on that vision means your team becomes a force that cannot be stopped.

WHY START WITH WHY?

Simon Sinek talks about the Golden Circle in his book, *Start with Why*. His Golden Circle is a set of three concentric circles, like a set of Russian dolls. **Why** is in the middle of the circle,

How is the next ring out and then **What** is the outermost circle. Most companies start with **What** they're going to do, then figure out **How** they'll do it, and maybe later come up with a fuzzy **Why** for their company.

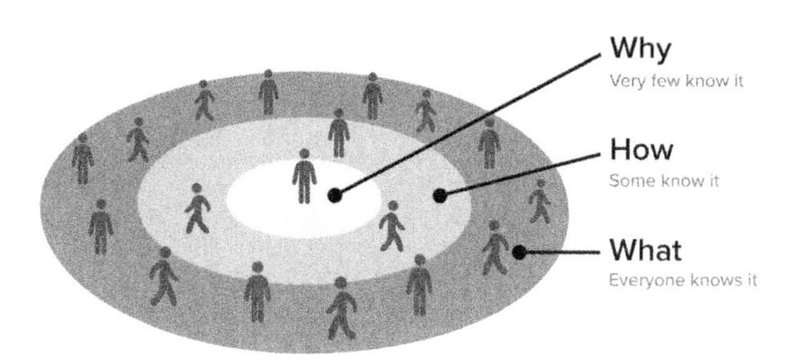

Sinek's favorite example of a company that starts with **Why** is Apple. Apple's **Why** is challenging the status quo and thinking differently. **How** they do it is by making products that are well-designed, easy to use, and with attention to design details. **What** they do is making computers and other electronics.

In contrast, most companies start with **What**. You see this a lot with companies that try to copy the business model of another successful company. Companies that only focus on **What** they do will be stuck just doing that, and **What** they do can easily become a commodity.

For FloQast, our **Why** is to help our clients close the books faster and more accurately. When we built our first product, I sat down with the team and explained what we were going to do, and showed them a mockup of what it would look like, and how it would work, and then why we were doing that.

Back then, I had all the accounting knowledge in the building, and so I needed to explain the **What, How** and **Why**. But it's very different today.

Today I reach behind that **Why** of closing the books faster and more accurately to a bigger **Why:** automate as much as possible. And behind that **Why** is an even bigger **Why:** in four or five years, we're going public, and we want our revenue to be homegrown with high net revenue retention numbers so that we can become very successful as a public company.

So for example, with the RPA we're building right now, because we want to automate as much as possible, this needs to be built in a way where it can roll out to customers on their own. Because my team understands why we're building it in a certain way, I can let my team figure out how to build it and what it should look like.

But what does your organization's **Why** have to do with the accounting department?

If you don't know where your organization is trying to go, you can't be of any help in achieving that goal.

A modern, strategic controller is doing more than just getting the numbers right every month. Even if that **Why** is just a tiny whisper in the back of your mind as you make your way through the interminable pile of work on your desk, your subconscious mind can be hard at work in the background.

Don't be surprised when you get sudden flashes of insight or when you find new and creative solutions that help you incorporate that **Why** into what you do every day.

Sharing that **Why** with others, and asking them to hold you accountable to it helps too. "It is helpful to have somebody pushing you to think bigger," said Chris Sluty, COO and co-founder of FloQast. "And when you do have the big goal, it's crazy how often you achieve that. Sometimes you've got to just put it out there and have that big goal to go towards and you figure it out along the way."

CULTURE = PEOPLE + TRUST + ACCOUNTABILITY

Here at FloQast, a bright mural near the bathrooms, right where everyone sees it multiple times every day, has these words in four-foot letters:

- Quality
- Passion
- Innovation
- Collaboration
- Integrity

These are the values that form the bedrock of our culture here. You might have different values at your organization. And as a controller, you might not have much impact on the values of your company or even on the long-term goals of the accounting department. But you can still create a culture for your team that will make achieving those long-term goals possible.

While every organization has values, not all organizations actually practice those values. In some organizations, those values may not be much more than a nicely framed piece of paper in the break room. The culture of your team or your company communicates what's most valued, and that drives their behavior.

So how do you create a culture that drives success in your organization? For decades, employee engagement has been thrown about as a magical cure-all that drives company success. The most recent iteration of Gallup's *State of the American Workplace*[3] notes a correlation between engaged employees and business success.

Gallup has been studying employee engagement for 15 years by looking at how well the performance development needs of employees across 12 dimensions are met. When an employer meets those needs, employees become "emotionally and psychologically attached to their work and workplace." In Gallup's latest meta-analysis of their survey results, they found the following:

> Business or work units that score in the top quartile of their organization in employee engagement have nearly double the odds of success (based on a composite of financial, customer retention, safety, quality, shrinkage, and absenteeism metrics) when compared with those in the

> bottom quartile. Those at the 99th percentile have four times the success rate of those at the first percentile.[4]

Now I agree that these survey results demonstrate a *correlation* between engaged employees and success for the company. This doesn't absolutely mean that engaged employees *cause* company success. But that's still a heckuva correlation. And it's a whole lot more enjoyable to work with engaged people than with actively disengaged people.

However, as Maddie Grant and Jamie Notter point out in their 2019 book, *The Non-Obvious Guide To Employee Engagement (For Millennials, Boomers And Everyone Else)*, for decades we've been looking at engagement the wrong way. We've been thinking of engagement in terms of making employees happy.

So we put in nice coffee bars, break rooms, and maybe foosball tables. We let employees bring their dogs to work. And so we've got slightly less unhappy employees. Many organizations make the mistake of doing an annual survey to monitor employee engagement, but nothing more.

Even after spending $1 billion a year on employee engagement programs for years, we don't see any material difference in employee engagement levels, which is borne out by the Gallup[5] survey results, which show that since 2000, the percentage of engaged employees has only increased from 26% to 33% in 2016.

Grant and Notter propose a different definition of employee engagement:

> Employee engagement is the level of emotional commitment and connection employees have to an organization, which is driven by how successful they are at work, both personally and organizationally. Employee

> engagement is the result of people being consistently successful. Period.

This makes sense from what I've experienced. Engaged employees aren't simply happy employees. Engagement is also about being challenged at work. And often, challenging someone is the opposite of making them "happy." If the focus is just on making employees happy, they might get bored, which is even worse for engagement.

By creating a workplace where team members can be successful in doing their work, we'll have engaged employees. Helping team members be successful means giving them the tools and technology they need, and helping them to see clearly how their work contributes to the Why of the company. Having engaged employees means success for employees and the company.

Grant and Notter's book, by the way, is a great resource for organizations and for individuals within organizations who want to increase the engagement level of their teams — or even themselves.

PEOPLE

"People are our greatest asset" has become a hackneyed and almost meaningless leadership maxim. That's because for years, this has just been lip service. EY said that, but like all the Big Four and most public accounting firms, they sure didn't treat us like their most valuable asset. In today's tight job market for accounting talent, any accountant who doesn't feel valued can easily find another job with the click of a mouse.

As Jim Collins says in his book *From Good to Great*, one of the keys for building a successful company is getting the right people doing the right things. "Good to great companies first got the right people on the bus—and the wrong people off the bus—and then figured out where to drive it."[6]

So what are the keys to getting the right people on your bus?

The first step is to hire the right people. I believe in hiring for attitude and potential. A candidate with a positive attitude and a desire to learn, but little relevant experience always trumps a candidate with years of experience, but who comes in with a big ego or a set way of thinking. As Herb Kelleher, founder of Southwest Airlines said, "You don't hire for skills, you hire for attitude. You can always teach skills."[7]

Today's work culture is changing, and the old-style, top-down, management-by-decree model of organizational leadership no longer works. The younger generations — and some of the older generations as well — want work that has meaning. They want to have input into how the company operates.

The best candidates don't want just a job. They want a company whose mission and vision is something they care about. They want to work for a company with a Why they can get behind.

Potential is meaningless, though, unless that diamond in the rough you hired wants to make the most of it. We've all worked with brilliant folks who were content to just coast on what they'd accomplished so far. So I look for a desire to learn. Not someone who's merely willing to learn, who is begrudgingly going to learn the minimum necessary to get the job done.

I used to work with a man who saw no reason to learn anything new unless it would have a direct impact on his ability to do his job. While he was brilliant, he didn't have a single innovative bone in his body. That's not the person you want.

Having a desire to learn means the candidate has a desire to get better as a human being, and that's going to inherently make that person a better employee. You want someone who doesn't need a carrot or a stick to learn. You want someone who's self-motivated to keep on making themselves better and who seeks continuous improvement.

With that being said, if you're hiring for a specialized role like SEC reporting, tax compliance, or internal audit, your best bet is to hire someone who's done this once before. In my opinion, the best practice is to hire someone who's only done this *once* to eliminate ego or a set way of thinking. These are complex, high risk areas, and hiring an amateur could lead to disaster.

TRUST

So you've made the right hires, and you trained them well. That means you can trust them to do their jobs and to do their jobs well.

This means those people are not required to be at their desk 8 to 5. Maybe your organization allows for remote work or flexible schedules, so it doesn't matter exactly when people are in the office or at work as long as they get their work done.

Being physically present, butt in the chair on a strict timetable, is only a requirement if you don't trust them to do the work or to do it correctly. This tells your team, "I don't trust you to work from home, so you've got to sit at your desk all day so that I can see you're getting stuff done." Lack of trust leads to micromanaging, and no one likes that.

A better option today is a flexible work schedule, where team members are not required to be present for set hours, but are generally available during some part of the work day, in some fashion for collaboration. Maybe that collaboration is on Slack or Teams or via text or Zoom meetings, but you need some method — and preferably just one main method — to get the group together and talk about current projects.

Just because someone's in the office doesn't mean you're necessarily going to trust them. They could still be doing their work improperly.

Presumably if you're hiring the right people, you don't need to babysit them and make sure they're doing the work. That's not an issue at all. And you've got to trust that when they run into problems, they feel comfortable asking for help. They need to know that asking for help isn't a sign of weakness but a sign of great strength, integrity, and efficiency. It's way better to ask for help than to twiddle your thumbs or spin your wheels and stay stuck.

Trust is two-way. Your people need to trust that you've got their back and that leadership wants what's best for them, even if that means moving to a different organization.

Trust also means they can be sure they'll be recognized for their ideas. The boss won't steal someone's idea and call it their own.

Review Note: Remote work vs. flexible work

Today's technology makes it easier than ever for people to work anywhere, anytime, and with any device. High speed internet, wifi everywhere, cloud software, and video conferencing mean that team members don't need to battle rush hour traffic just to be at the office from 8 to 5 every day.

Remote work means team members can work from anywhere in the world that has an internet connection. That might be occasionally working from home so they can avoid a long commute or care for a family member. Or maybe the best candidate for the job lives too far away to make it feasible to work in the office.

Flexible work is a broad category that simply means team members don't have to be physically present in the office during set hours every day. Every organization defines this differently. At one end of the spectrum, employees might be able to shift their starting and ending times, and perhaps come in at nine instead of eight, and leave at six instead of five. But they still need to put in eight hours a day, 40 hours a week.

Some organizations let employees set their own work schedules for times they'll be in the office or work from home. Maybe this will be four 10-hour days instead of five eight-hour days. Maybe they'll work more hours early in the month to get the close done, and fewer later in the month. Flexible hours might also include remote work for some or all of the work. Some organizations establish "core work hours" that they expect most people to be available for collaboration and to answer questions.

Organizations might set a fixed number of hours every week that they expect team members to put in, and how they arrange those hours is up to the employee. At the other extreme of the spectrum for flexible work, an organization might have no requirements for how many hours a team member needs to put in as long as they get their work done.

Here at FloQast, our team leaders establish expectations. I like having everyone in the same building at least part of the time because that makes collaboration easy, when you can just walk down the hall and grab someone for a quick one-on-one in one of our conference rooms. And because we don't keep our teams separated in silos, that contact with different parts of the company means we find creative and non-obvious solutions that come from collaborating with people from different backgrounds.

But our team leaders also recognize that some people prefer to spend some time working at home or in their favorite productive space so they can put their head down and get the work done without interruption. Some folks come in early, some stay late. Some spend part of their days at home, and part in the office. Whatever schedule helps them to be successful at their job is the best schedule for that person.

The keys to making remote work and flexible work successful are trust and accountability. You've got to trust that your employees are committed to getting their work done. They're not just clocking in and out for a paycheck. You can't have any kind of judgment that when someone leaves at 3 PM, they're slacking off and not working on what they need to.

Accountability is what develops that trust. When you can see that team members are hitting their deadlines and are getting their work done at a high level of quality, then it's easier to trust that whatever schedule they're on is the right one for them.

MCW

ACCOUNTABILITY

The old definition of accountability is being held to performance standards by your direct supervisor. But the new definition is being held to a standard by the members of your team. Transparency is the only way that works. Everybody has to see what everyone else is working on to function as a team.

Being accountable means establishing goals and assigning owners at every level in the organization, then checking in and making sure the work to accomplish those goals is getting done. This is best modeled from the top down when you make public commitments and meet them. When you take ownership of any mistakes, and take full responsibility for them without blaming someone else or something outside of you.

Transparency enables accountability by requiring people to tell you what they're going to do and when they're going to get it done. Following up to make sure the work gets done closes the loop. If you don't follow up, accountability is nothing more than wishful thinking.

A good example of accountability is the gymnastics team for the Olympics. The members compete individually, but they train together. Because they train together, they're both supportive and accountable to each other.

We designed the FloQast dashboard with transparency and accountability in mind. Everyone can see which tasks are assigned to which people, and whether those tasks have been completed or not. And with the documentation just a click away, it's ridiculously easy to verify that the work has been done. Our Review Notes also keep everyone on the same page, so that everyone can see questions and answers to those questions.

TECHNOLOGY = PROCESS + TOOLS + KNOWLEDGE

Before I delve into the components of this last equation, let me talk about the misconception that implementing the latest technology tool will fix everything that ails an organization. This is wishful, magical thinking. We've all heard about — or maybe even seen firsthand — how putting the latest and greatest tech on top of a dysfunctional organization just makes that organization dysfunctional in faster and more complex ways.

So before you start looking at tech tools, take a step back and look at your whole organization. Maybe through your leadership as a modern controller you can make the accounting department a better place, even if the rest of the organization isn't optimal. Maybe you're fortunate and have a great C-suite team that wants to build a best-in-class organization. Or maybe your organization suffers from poor leadership, and there's not much anyone can do about it until (or if) the tone from the top changes.

TECHNOLOGY

Without technology, we'd still be using those green 10-column ledgers and 10-keys. In today's rapidly changing world, keeping up with the technology in accounting is becoming harder and harder. In our survey of finance professionals,[8] 69% of the 202 controllers who responded said that the speed of technology changes is contributing to the evolution of the role of the controller. And controllers are increasingly leading the charge to update technology at their organizations.

Some technology just updates current processes by automating what used to be done manually. This kind of technology complements what we as humans already do. Other technology imagines completely new ways to do the work. This type of technology will radically change how controllers work.

RPA, AI, machine learning, blockchain, data visualization, and data analytics are all becoming real parts of the tech we can use today. While I can't predict what controllers will be using in the future, I can predict that in a few years, what is cutting-edge today will be hopelessly outdated.

Out in the real world, futurists are predicting that things like car keys, light switches, TVs, and cash will be obsolete in the next few decades, if not sooner. Tablets will take the place of laptops and desktops. Cloud storage will replace flash drives. Driverless cars will be the norm.

Technology is making it easier for everyone to access information. Advanced reporting tools mean you no longer have to be fluent in SQL to extract insights from your ERP. And it also means that others across your organization no longer need to depend on you to get them the reports and data they need to do their jobs. Do-it-yourself dashboards bring that information directly to the people who need it.

Easy access to more accurate information in almost real time means that CEOs and CFOs can make decisions based on real numbers, not just their gut instinct. Trusting intuition can still be a good thing, but now, it's not the only thing leaders have to rely on.

Innovation in accounting technology means that the insights from better, faster information and analytics on that data are available to more people, and to many for the first time. It's no longer a luxury but an expectation. As the Susskinds write in *The Future of the Professions,* innovation across the professions is "providing access where there has previously been unmet demand."[9]

Because of technology, we're swimming in a sea of data, which means we need even more technology to manage that data. DOMO estimates that by 2020, 1.7 MB of data will be created every second for every person on earth.[10] In 2016, Deloitte predicted that by 2025,[11] finance will be changing from transaction processing to "design, configuration, and maintenance of systems."

So if you're not already working to bring technology into your workflow, it will only become worse if you don't. If your competition is beating you to the punch, they could run you out of business.

Controllers are the ones who are driving technical innovation in their companies. At the very least, they need to be actively involved in the selection and implementation of the technology they use. Here at FloQast, we take that a step further by actively recruiting accountants to join our team so that we have accountants involved in the development of the technology that other accountants will use. Right now, we have 38 accountants at FloQast, spread across every department, from engineering to marketing. About half of them are CPAs.

But before you ask "What tech should I implement?" consider what the business needs. What kinds of information will the business as a whole and by department need to compete successfully?

WHAT APPS DO WE USE AT FLOQAST?

The rise of cloud technology and apps means we no longer need an in-house coder to create bespoke solutions. There are plenty of automation tools on the market already that you can use to create big wins.

Choosing best-of-breed cloud solutions means you don't have to worry about updates to the latest version or installing the latest security patches. It's done for you. Here's a visual of the tech stack we were using at FloQast in the summer of 2019:

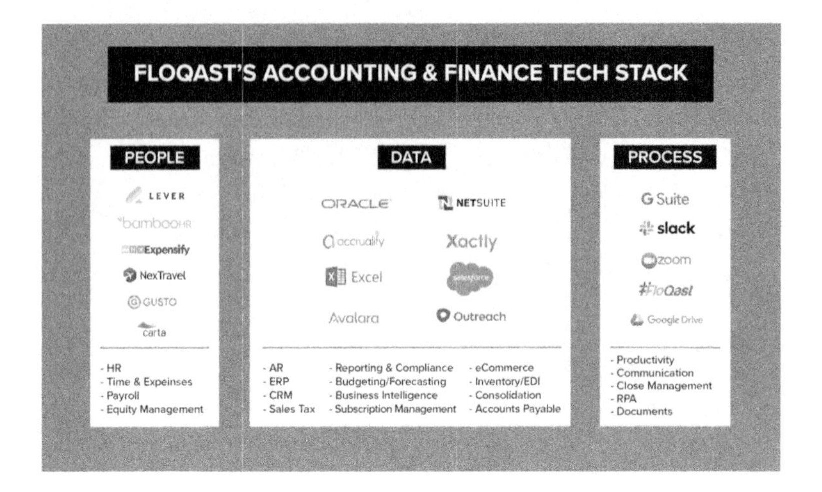

PROCESS

Besides automating your processes with technology, standardizing and optimizing them is the most important work you need to do. One of my CPA friends told me about an HVAC client she was working with. Their process for approving invoices for payment required almost every person in a 12-member accounting department plus the three owners to touch every invoice at least once, and sometimes three times.

Although they were reluctant to change, the HVAC company owners agreed that only the owner who served as CFO needed to be part of the process. Next, they implemented a one-touch process for approving invoices which put an end to the confusing back-and-forth shuffle of papers. Just by making those small changes — and not even adding a tool like Bill.com — that HVAC company was able to speed up vendor payments by a full week, and when two junior accountants left, they didn't need to hire anyone to replace those missing team members.

Michael Gerber introduced many business owners to systems through his E-Myth series. The basic idea behind those books is to develop standard processes and systems for everything as if you were going to franchise your business. So a hotel, for example, might develop scripts and processes for all of the interactions with hotel guests. These processes are what set the experience at a Hilton Hotel apart from the experience at a Comfort Inn. They're part of why a guest is willing to spend five or six times as much for the same basic service: a private room with a bed and a bathroom.

For controllers, developing standard processes and optimizing them can help streamline the regular monthly activities of your work. Even before you add tools like FloQast, establishing standard processes and documenting them can lead to huge efficiency gains.

When you develop standard processes for recurring tasks, you make it possible to delegate work, or to move tasks around to different people. With processes, and some kind of dashboard tool to monitor progress on completing tasks, it's no longer a disaster when a key person isn't available.

On a recent FloQast webinar,[12] Amy Knust, Senior Manager at Eide Bailly, recommended that when configuring user roles in NetSuite, a best practice is to figure out the different roles on your team, and configure the user roles by the actual roles. Configuring the user roles based on the individuals and what that person does today can make it challenging if that person leaves or if those tasks are moved to another person.

Similarly, you can define your team by the roles they will fill on your team. Then you can hire for the specific skills needed for that role, and not by some arbitrary criteria. Hiring someone because they spent two years as a Big Four auditor doesn't always get you the skills or the attitude they need to be an effective member of your team.

This modular, systems-based approach also allows you to

move people around as needed. Plus it makes scaling your team much easier. This may mean that the traditional job titles of senior accountant or accounting manager may no longer be as relevant as they used to be.

In a similar fashion, sports teams have players who fulfill roles. Football teams have receivers and quarterbacks and linebackers. Those roles don't diminish the players as people, and don't limit their creativity in fulfilling those roles, but it gives each player a framework for what they do.

The next step after developing your processes is to make them into checklists. Most accountants LOVE checklists! Some accountants prefer keeping those processes in their heads. But as Atul Gawande explains in his book Checklist Manifesto, checklists free up your brain so you can focus on what matters:

> The fear people have about the idea of adherence to protocol is rigidity. They imagine mindless automatons, heads down in a checklist, incapable of looking out their windshield and coping with the real world in front of them. But what you find, when a checklist is well made, is exactly the opposite. The checklist gets the dumb stuff out of the way, the routines your brain shouldn't have to occupy itself with.

THE IMPORTANCE OF DOCUMENTING HOW TO DO THE WORK

As every organization develops standard processes for doing the work, just having a list of tasks in a checklist may not be sufficient. Someone who has always reconciled a certain account knows that a specific report has to be run, with certain parameters, but that's not documented anywhere. Traditionally, this almost top-secret, tribal knowledge was passed down, person to person, almost as a rite of passage to the next level.

But what if the current secret keeper walks out the door, or can't do their job this month because of a family emergency? This leaves everyone else scrambling to pick up the pieces. And it also makes it hard to shift tasks around to even out everyone's workload.

Some people jealously hoard this information as a means to hold on to some illusory sense of power. This attitude has no place in today's workplace, and people like this need to be shown the door.

Documenting your team's tribal knowledge means your team can grow, adapt and change. Sharing this information means an end to bottlenecks because everyone is waiting for a particular task to be completed. By writing it down and making it public, others can make sure that the process is correct and up to date. Processes can be tweaked and updated as needed. Maybe it can be used elsewhere in your processes or elsewhere in your organization.

A best practice we recommend is to save that documentation by account or process and date, not by the person doing the work.

By documenting everything about how you do the work, you'll have freedom you thought wasn't possible.

Take a look at the case study below to learn how a controller at a tech company took a 10-week vacation. Yes, 10 weeks.

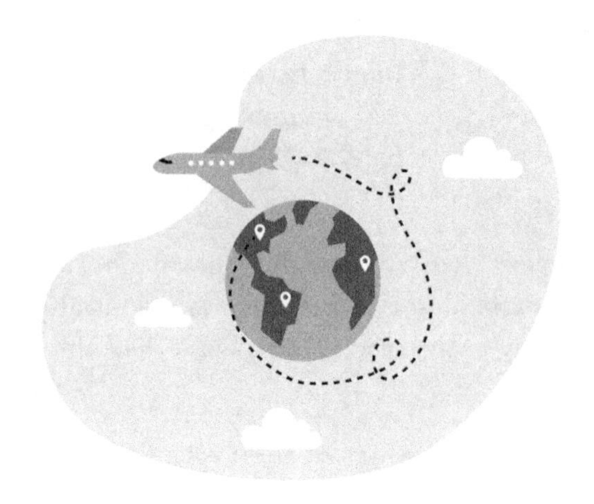

Case Study: The controller who took 10 weeks off to travel the world

The former controller at Stack Overflow was the first person the company hired in accounting. This person did everything at first. She hired and developed a small team. They built the processes and procedures they needed, so she was able to delegate some of her responsibilities. When Stack Overflow started using FloQast, she documented everything inside of the platform.

After being in the role for over two years, the controller took advantage of the Stack Overflow sabbatical program and traveled the world for two and a half months. During this time, she used her travel adventures to grow her own experience and came back with new ideas for the team.

I asked Stack Overflow's CFO, Jerry Raphael, "How did you feel about the all-star on your team disappearing for 10 weeks?" His response was positive, given the work the controller had done in ensuring process and policies were well documented. He said, "Well, she documented everything really well, she hired really good people, and we were able to pick up the workload while she was gone seamlessly. It actually worked out really well and the team continued to provide a strong support function to the broader Stack Overflow operations."

As this story demonstrates, FloQast is a great place to store the tribal knowledge about your accounting processes. But what about the rest of your organization?

Here at FloQast, we built these Google Sites to preserve that tribal knowledge. Our product and engineering teams use Confluence to document all of their decisions. I find it pretty fascinating to go in and trace their thinking when they're pushing out a new product feature.

SLOW AND STEADY IMPROVEMENT IS MORE SUSTAINABLE

Don't uproot all your processes, but iterate. Make incremental changes instead of drastic ones, and then repeat, to make those incremental changes better. This is like learning to crawl and walk before you run.

Remember, water wears away stone. An incremental and patient approach will get you there, and will most likely be better and more sustainable than a slash-and-burn approach. That just leads to resistance and resentment.

TOOLS

Software is the main tool you use as a controller. But without the other two pieces of this equation — processes and knowledge — you risk failure.

A commonly tossed around stat is that half of all ERP implementations fail.[13] However, a survey performed in late 2018 by Mint Jutras[14] found instead that 67% of the 315 distributors and manufacturers they surveyed deemed their ERP implementation either "successful" or "very successful." But of those respondents who did not rate their ERP implementation as at least "successful," 31% cited "Inadequate Business Process Re-Engineering" as a primary cause of failure. A mismatch between processes and software isn't just annoying — it can cause implementation failures.

Digging further into the results, the survey authors noted that while technological improvements over the last few years have made ERP implementation much less painful than it used to be, it seems that companies have underestimated the potential benefits of their new system.

When asked to select all of the benefits of their new system from a list of 10 benefits, including such items as "Improved data availability/accessibility" and "Employees experience improved personal productivity", respondents selected an average of fewer than three. "We suspect that many, upon going live, breathe a collective sigh of relief and go back to business as usual," said the survey authors. "They don't set the bar high enough in terms of the return on their investment, and they don't even try to make those returns sustainable."

As mentioned above, adding new tools may require some "Business Process Re-Engineering." But the best tools — and new processes — are created with the needs of the users in mind. Software engineers who try to change a process they've never been a part of might fail, and especially when they try to prescribe the ways the users now have to do their work.

That's why we designed FloQast around Excel — the favorite tool of accountants. Unlike our competitors, we don't force you to use unfamiliar and poorly functioning webforms.

Then there's the software where you fall for the demo, but never implement it, so it ends up on your shelf. I call that shelfware.

The future will be humans working alongside machines. This will require different skill sets. Millennials and members of Generation Z won't have any problems picking up those skills because they grew up with technology. But it may be a challenge for older team members. So maybe you'll pair up a tech-savvy youngster with an older business- and finance-savvy team member and see what they can teach each other.

KNOWLEDGE

The third crucial component for maximizing your return on any technology your organization implements is knowledge. If you were a former auditor like me, you know GAAP (and maybe IFRS as well) inside and out. But that's not the only kind of knowledge you need to help your organization achieve its goals.

In my mind, there are two types of knowledge that need to become part of the shared intellectual capital of your organization.

1. **How to do the work**. This is what many refer to as "tribal knowledge:" the crucial information about how to get your systems to work together and how to get the information you need for your regular work out of your systems.
2. **Why we do the work**. This includes the Why for your organization and your department, as well as all of the anecdotal information about why your organization has chosen product or service A over product or service B. Central to this type of knowledge is understanding your customers so you can serve them better.

We talked a lot about the first type of knowledge in the section on processes. Getting a handle on this type of knowledge requires you to have your processes defined, optimized, aligned with your tech, clearly documented, and out of the domain of tribal knowledge. A high-performing accounting department willingly and freely shares the knowledge of how to do the work among all team members.

Review Note: What is intellectual capital?

As Ron Baker describes in his book, *Measure What Matters to Customers: Using Key Predictive Indicators,* intellectual capital is the intangible value of an organization. It's not on the balance sheet. But it can be the most valuable asset of an organization. Intellectual capital is composed of:

- **Human capital -** what the employees know
- **Relational or social capital -** relationships with customers, vendors, referral sources, and others
- **Structural capital -** everything that's left after the employees go home

Human capital can be increased by hiring people with the skills your organization needs, by helping existing employees improve their skills and knowledge, and by using more of what they already know.

Relational capital grows when you provide good customer service, and when you treat your vendors fairly. It also grows as your company's profile elevates to become a great company.

Structural capital is all the knowledge about how to do the work that may be already documented in your files somewhere. But it doesn't include the tribal knowledge that resides only in the heads of a select few people. By developing mechanisms to capture the learning, you help to increase the structural capital of your organization.

WHY WE DO THE WORK

Modern controllers are no longer just focused on the debits and credits. They don't spend their days hiding in an office, creating that Excel masterpiece. They get out in their organizations and talk to others to understand how the business works. They're continually expanding their understanding of the second type of knowledge of their organizations — why they do the work. The Why of the accounting department and the Why of the organization are the guidelines to keep them focused on their top priorities.

Having a big picture view of your whole organization is a must for the modern controller. You have to establish relationships with other parts of your organization. Find out ways that finance can help them do their job better. You also need to understand where your organization fits in its marketplace. What are your competitors doing that's better or worse than what your organization is doing?

WHAT IS THE ACCOUNTING TEAM'S NET PROMOTER SCORE?

The Net Promoter Score is a metric to measure the loyalty of a company's customers. This is calculated by asking customers just one question: One a scale of 1 to 10, how likely are you to recommend this company to others?

Customers who answer with a 9 or 10 are promoters, 7 or 8 are the passives, and 1 - 6 are the detractors. Subtract the percentage of detractors from the percentage of promoters to get your net promoter score.

For example, if 50% of respondents are promoters and 20% are detractors, the Net Promoter Score is 30%.

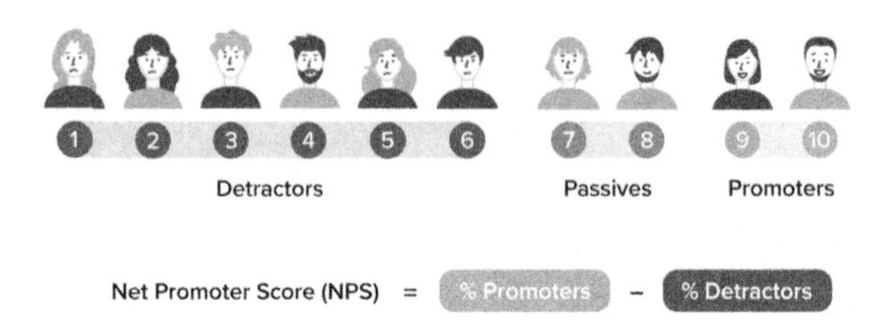

A colleague told me that he heard Amy Vetter, CPA, CGMA, CITP speak at the AICPA Controllers' Conference about using Net Promoter Score to gauge what your company thinks about the accounting department.

If the only contact someone in marketing has with the accountants is constant requests for information, they'll probably rank accounting firmly in the detractor range.

But if you're constantly asking the head of marketing what information she needs from accounting to do a better job, and following up by delivering that information in an easily digestible format, she might give you a 9 or 10. Having those conversations is huge in building relational capital.

Today's technology makes it easier than ever to extract information from your ERP, then marry it to your CRM, and pop all of that into a visualization tool so that the insights buried in it jump right out.

What do you think others in your company will think of the accounting department?

TRANSFORMING ACCOUNTING, ONE CONTROLLER AT A TIME

Here at FloQast, our Why doesn't just stop at helping accountants close the books faster and more accurately. We also want to be part of the financial transformation that's impacting all parts of the accounting and finance world. The technology we're creating is just a part of helping controllers get out of the mundane processes like the close, and empowering them so they can be more strategic in their jobs.

Transforming accounting means building a new foundation. Our big Why at FloQast is to be one of the big columns that makes up that foundation. This framework I'm laying out here will help those controllers who want to move up in their careers.

The future is going to be interesting for the controllers who want to become more strategic in their roles. The controller's job is to oversee all of accounting, and whatever relates to getting numbers up to the VP of finance or the CFO. Their job will be dictated by what happens within the industry.

There's always going to be new guidance that comes out that they have to stay up to date on. Controllers will always have to be able to manage a team. They have to be able to understand and review numbers. That's how the job of controller has been for decades.

But now, the other new thing they're having to learn is technology. That's going to become a bigger and bigger part of the future. Not just how IT at large plays into their department but also across the entire business function.

I think that's going to be the area where controllers are really going to need to stay up to date on how things work. Any controller today who knows enough to be dangerous about NetSuite administration, for example, is going to be in a much better position than someone who doesn't know anything about the future.

But just nailing the technology part isn't the only thing controllers have to master. In our framework, Success is made up of Culture plus Technology. Culture is made up of People plus Trust plus Accountability. Technology is made up of Process plus Tools plus Knowledge.

None of this is generally taught alongside the debits and credits and FASB and IFRS guidance we have to learn in school. It's not part of the CPA exam.

So in this book, I'm aiming to point you towards the additional areas of mastery you'll need so you can be strategic in your career and strategic as a leader in your organization. With this framework, I'll help you address two of the biggest challenges for controllers today: building a first-class team in an era when the unemployment rate for accountants is basically zero, and mitigating risk across your organization.

PART 2
THE PEOPLE PROBLEM

3 / WHY ARE PEOPLE SUCH A PROBLEM?

People are more difficult to work with than machines. And when you break a person, he can't be fixed.
– Rick Riordan

The nature of work is changing, and those changes will have a direct impact on the people on your team and how you lead them. Automation, robotics, AI, RPA, and machine learning, along with generational changes in attitudes about work are creating seismic shifts in the workplace worldwide. The "one job for life" that our grandparents had is a quaint, distant memory. And going into an office Monday through Friday from 9 to 5 is quickly becoming an anachronism as well. The future will be humans augmented by automation, working in a variety of locations, likely on flexible schedules.

According to a McKinsey report from 2017,[1] automation has the potential to drastically change occupations worldwide. Some occupations will disappear completely. More than half of all workplaces will automate 30% or more of the activities people do today. However, if the pattern of past technological disruptions holds true, new occupations will be created that don't exist today and which we can't even imagine.

This isn't a new phenomenon. Think of what email, voice mail, and messaging apps did to legions of secretaries and administrative assistants who used to handle business correspondence just 20 or 30 years ago. Or consider the impact of the electronic spreadsheet in the 1980s and 90s. Hundreds of thousands of accounts preparation jobs were eliminated, but even more accounting jobs were created.

Even today, these changes are creating shortages in jobs that didn't exist a few years ago. A 2018 survey by McKinsey Global Institute of more than 3,000 C-level executives around the world found that the largest skill shortages are in the areas of data analytics, IT/mobile/web design, and R&D.[2]

Research by the World Bank found that valued skills in the future will be "a combination of technological know-how, problem-solving, and critical thinking, as well as soft skills such as perseverance, collaboration, and empathy."[3] These are the kinds of skills that machines don't do well.

Those findings echo what McKinsey Global Institute determined when they used the data from their 2017 survey to develop a model to predict the changes in the workforce in

2030.[4] According to that model, the most important skills of the future will be technological skills, social and emotional skills, and higher level cognitive skills.

The good news for controllers is that these advances in technology mean the boring stuff is mostly going away. Within a decade, much of the routine work we do will be automated or done by bots.

But what that means is that many entry level, low skill jobs in accounting will go away. Some of those people can be retrained to do higher level work, but those who can't or won't may face a bleak future. But for those who can adapt, the future is bright.

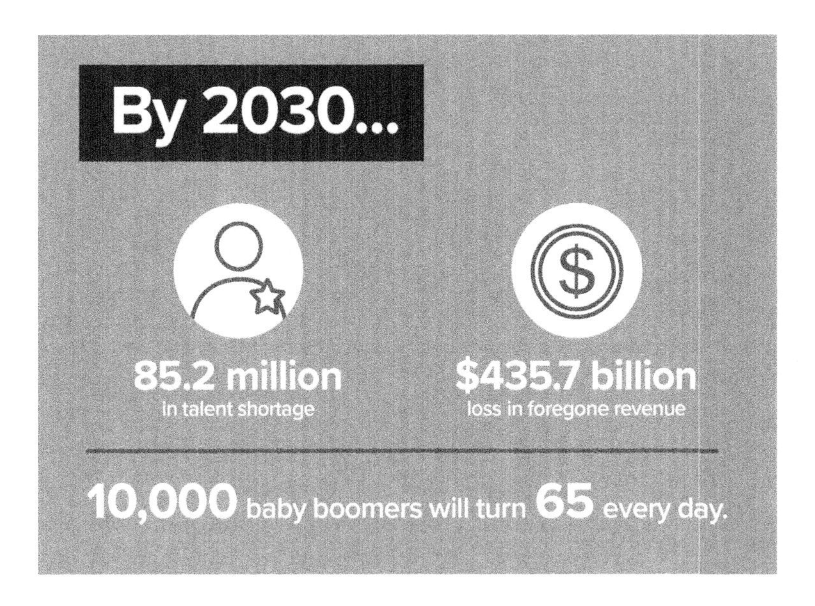

Researchers at Korn Ferry[5] predict that by 2030, there will be a global talent shortage of 85.2 million people. In the U.S., the shortage of talent in the financial and business sectors could mean a loss of as much as $435.7 billion in foregone revenue in 2030. This is 1.5% of the entire U.S. economy. Part of this shortage is caused by a massive wave of Baby Boomers reaching retirement age. Since January 1, 2011, and continuing until 2030, 10,000 Baby Boomers will turn 65 every day.[6]

Besides the impending retirement of Baby Boomers, our increasingly technical world requires more and more highly skilled workers, and our education programs, which were designed for a different era, aren't keeping up.

Automation will help, as researchers at the Brookings Institution describe in a recent study.[7] Automation won't replace jobs exactly, but it will take over many of the tasks of certain jobs, so that fewer people may be needed to fulfill the responsibilities of some occupations. However, as the authors of the Brookings Institution study and the Korn Ferry study point out, the solution to both the shortage of highly-skilled talent and the displacement of workers by automation and AI will be retraining and up-skilling workers for the kinds of jobs that robots can't do.

For those who already have the kinds of high-level skills that will be in demand, such as the technical financial skills that controllers already have, your future employment prospects are excellent. And if you continue to grow your skills and knowledge in areas like data analytics, you'll be even more valuable to your company.

At the same time that we're facing a talent crunch, due in part to retiring Baby Boomers, and due in part to the workforce skills needed as low level tasks and jobs are automated out of existence, the workplace is also getting pressure from the Millennial generation to change to a new way of working.

My generation has been called entitled and spoiled. Older folks complain that we're not willing to pay our dues. But what's really happening is more complex than an entitled generation. We grew up with tech, so we'd rather find a tech tool to do the work than do it manually.

We also grew up in an information-rich world, where it was just as easy to read news from India as from our home town, and where the choices for getting information and entertainment weren't limited to the four channels on broadcast TV. We're connected to friends and communities all over the world. Our view of the world doesn't end at the edge of town.

This broader view makes us more inclined to just call BS on things we see that aren't working.

This perfect storm of talent shortage, automation, and generational shifts means that solving the people problem will take more than just throwing more money at it. Controllers will have to consider a bigger approach, something that few of us were taught in school. You'll have to work on the culture part of success.

Remember our second equation...

Culture = People + Trust + Accountability

Let's take a look at the elements of this to see how this can help us solve the people problem.

4 / CULTURE IS THE KEY

Customers will never love a company until the employees love it first.
–Simon Sinek

As I mentioned in the last section, our values are painted on the wall by our bathrooms, the part of the building that everyone passes by multiple times every day. Quality. Passion. Innovation. Collaboration. Integrity. A lot of companies do something like that, but if those values aren't part of the fabric of the workplace, it's just a nice decoration, or maybe a pretty framed document on the break room wall.

Putting words on the wall is one thing. Seeing that played out in our team is another. Here's what some FloQast team members say about working here:

My co-founder Cullen Zandstra is intrigued by the way accounting and engineering collide:

> *It's always exciting when you're taking a new approach to old problems. And that's exactly what we're doing. We are looking at problems that have existed for a long time, and we're asking ourselves, Is there a better way to do this? A more intuitive way? You know, is there a way that we can challenge preconceived notions? We can challenge the status quo and we can break the mold. And I think that that type of thinking is exciting no matter what you're doing.*
>
> *And we're really looking to that feeling of innovation. We're building something that is going to disrupt what is currently thought to be the way to do things. And I think that confluence of bringing really smart people that have the accounting background and have the engineering background, and intermingling them together, and asking them to challenge what is currently out there, and to come up with new ideas, I think that that just breeds excitement. And if you give smart, creative people an opportunity and a platform to be smart and creative, I think that is the crux of the excitement around the office.*

Shivang Patel, Director of Sales Engineering, spent several years in public accounting before he was hired as Accounting Manager at a Bay Area tech company. Now you can spot him in his Golden State Warriors hat and a T-shirt, or look for the dude jamming out to Styx early in the morning:

> *Obviously we do have business etiquette, we're professionals. But we also like to have fun. I feel like I can be 100% myself here. And I feel valued and respected. These days, people come to me for direction, advice, and guidance, and I love that.*

> *I used to sell deals, and traditionally what a sales person gets pride off of is getting that signed agreement. But for me it didn't matter as much. What meant more to me than the signed contract was when I taught somebody something, and they applied it, and the look on their face when they told me "Shivang, thank you so much for telling me that, here's how it worked." And I continuously get that feeling and that vibe here.*

Adey Tadesse-Heath, Director of HR, sees the way we've built a culture that supports success from the top down:

> *The feedback we've gotten from candidates and visitors is that right when you walk in there's that energy of everybody wanting to work really hard. The original crew, the OG folks, really don't have even a single ounce of one-upmanship in them. Now those people are all in higher positions. So when new folks come on board, they look up to those people who started where they are now and they think "I want to get to where you are. I want to duplicate your success."*
>
> *And so not only do they follow the work practices, but they also follow the behavioral practices of our leaders. They see that the leaders are all nice people, so they say "I'm gonna be a nice person, too." Because when you see other people who are very successful, but they're not the nicest people, other people think that that's what it takes to be successful. So I think it's our original folks who are now leading and mentoring the newer folks by keeping those core values, and living them for real.*

Chris Sluty spent eight years doing audit in public accounting firms before I convinced him to join me and Cullen at FloQast as a co-founder. One of his most impactful mentors was an audit partner who was always questioning why the team was doing something that didn't add value. He applies that mindset to helping his team innovate:

If you give people opportunities to own things that maybe their title doesn't say they should be running point on this project, but they're passionate about it, then they're going to really, really care because they're making changes here. They're the boots on the ground. They're the most intimate with our internal process. They know how to fix things. And sure, I've got some good ideas, but if somebody's going to execute on a vision, they've got to be bought in on it. So I think the big thing for us is giving people opportunities.

Hey, everybody's got good ideas. And if you've got a good idea, don't just sit on it. An idea is nothing without execution. So I think it's really about just giving everybody a voice. And if somebody's passionate about something, I think it's really important to give them the opportunity to take on that project.

Greg Vecellio, Controller at FloQast, spent several years as the assistant North America controller for a large global company. He remembers the hellish chaos that was the close, a marathon of long days with a tight and unforgiving deadline. Greg's office, like all the offices at FloQast, has a large window looking out across the building and he sees a parade of people all day:

I see people all day collaborating. People come over here and talk to the security people, then security's going over there and talking with engineering. Sales is coming back and talking to engineering. So there is a very collaborative process here. If you've got an issue, or if you have an idea, all you have to do is identify the person you need to bring it to, and you can bring it to them. People are very open and receptive.

I think it is a very special place here. I think there is a genuine openness here, and a genuine level of mutual respect for everybody, for people's ideas and for them as individuals. I've never heard anybody make a snide comment. That just doesn't happen here. You don't find that in a lot of places.

One of the perks of building a company from the ground up is that you get to create the kind of workplace that you want to work in. And as lame as it sounds, people do love the perks like snacks in the kitchen. But it's really about creating meaning at work, and having people feel like they want to show up and do something every day.

Creating this kind of culture doesn't happen overnight. It takes work and commitment. You have to be willing to always want to model the right behaviors as Adey said. You have to be willing to try doing things differently, as Cullen said, and you have to be willing to let people execute on their ideas, as Chris said. And most important, as Shivang said, the impact your company has on its customers has to be more important than the monetary rewards.

Every one of us has either worked at a place with a bad culture, or has heard horror stories from friends. The building block of company culture is the team, but how do you build great teams? I always played a lot of sports growing up, so I've always looked to teams as a way to create something bigger than the individual.

WHAT TEAM ARE YOU ON?

Back when I was at Cornerstone, initially there wasn't much understanding of how to build a team. They were just hiring lots of Big Four auditors to fill out the accounting department without really considering where in an org chart someone would fit.

Big Four accountants are naturally pretty competitive, so there was this weird dynamic around who was going to get promoted next. And frankly, a lot of the work that we were doing really didn't need a Big Four auditor to do it. So we had frustration that we weren't doing the kind of work that our credentials said we should. There wasn't much of a team feeling. It was more that we ought to be happy just to be working at this great company.

As I've discovered innately in building a company, that's exactly the wrong attitude to have. And the research backs me up on this. Marcus Buckingham and Ashley Goodall took a deep dive into the commonly held beliefs about work using data from thousands of employee surveys from the Gallup organization and Cisco. They found that many of the leadership and management notions we're taught as gospel truth just ain't so. Instead, these are lies, which they compiled in a book called *Nine Lies About Work: A Freethinking Leader's Guide to the Real World.* This book, by the way, should be part of your curriculum on becoming a better leader.

Number one on their list of lies is "People care which company they work for." Instead, they found that

> People care which team they're on." Your team is the most important aspect of your workplace. As the authors say, "If we put you in a good team at a bad company, you'll tend to hang around, but if we put you in a bad team at a good company, you won't be there for long. The team is the sun, the moon, and the stars of your experience at work.[1]

Buckingham and Goodall found that people on teams were twice as likely to be engaged at work. Further, they found that people who trust their team leaders were twelve times as likely to be engaged. They also found that the culture of a particular team — how people work and talk to each other — was vastly more important than any perks companies offer.

As a controller, you might not have much input into the kinds of perks your company offers, but those perks are much less important than how you lead your team. As Buckingham and Goodall say:

> You might not be able to weigh in on your company's parental-leave policy, or the quality of its cafeteria, but you can build a healthy team—you can set clear expectations for your people, or not; you can position each person to play to his or her strengths every day, or not; you can praise the team for excellent work, or not; you can help people grow their careers, or not. And you can, over time, build trust with your people, or not. Of course, given the "always-on" nature of your daily work, attending to each of these is challenging, but at least they are indeed part of your daily work.[2]

Chris Sluty, CPO here at FloQast, is doing just that. Here's what he says about how he leads his team:

The way I interact with my team is by empowering them. I don't need to make every single decision. This is a team sport. We're all trying to achieve goals on the close together. And if you take on that burden yourself it's going to be overwhelming. So the more that you're working with your team through challenges, giving them a voice so you understand exactly what those bottlenecks are and how to improve, with that, you can really become the visionary.

BUILDING A TEAM GIVES YOU THE TIME TO BE STRATEGIC

If you're always in the weeds of the debits and credits, you don't have the mental bandwidth or the time to take on a more strategic role. Derek Mernagh, Controller at Yelp, offers this advice on the importance of building a good team, and how that can help you in your career:

> *What I'd say is most important to give yourself more time to be*

strategic for the business is really about hiring the right team under you. The day-to-day operation of an effective accounting department really needs to have strong leaders, both in accounting and accounting operations.

I have learned, personally, over the years that it's so important to hire well, and also to structure the team in such a way that if someone leaves, or if there are changes within the department, that doesn't become your problem. You never want to be in that position where you're having to pick up the slack of that person leaving.

And I've found that that's a really effective way for me to remove myself from the day-to-day. Obviously, I get involved in the key areas that I think are really important, like making sure that I'm up to speed on what's going on with each month end close, make sure that I'm up to speed with our SEC filings and any other reporting that we do. And internally, keeping up to speed on any issues that escalate to me, and how they're remediated. And when you're in a position where you've removed yourself as much as possible from the day-to-day grind, then you can be more strategic.

And I think that's really the way you see progression in your career: when you can sit in meetings with other teams in the business and add value, and give the accounting perspective. And I think if you're not in those types of meetings, and you're not given an opportunity to do that, then you've probably got to look at how you structured your team and how you can extract yourself to be able to be more strategic.

I've been able to be more strategic in engaging more with FP&A by giving them guidance on how they can forecast certain areas that involve a lot of judgments. I also work with Investor Relations, and how they are selling the message of the company. I work with business partners as well to add value to what they're working on from the controller perspective. I think the controller has a unique insight into expenditures and other trends in the business.

And once you have the day-to-day bread and butter in place, and you have the team in place to do that, then you can extract yourself out of those activities and be more strategic.

BUILD A COLLABORATIVE CULTURE

Today's tech and the pace of change means accountants can't work in isolation anymore. The future will be more collaboration across teams and across parts of the business. To build that, you need to hire people who have a team orientation, and who aren't happiest spending days in a corner cube working on that spreadsheet masterpiece (which no one will look at anyways). You want people who aren't afraid to ask questions when they need help, and who are willing to help each other out, because they trust each other implicitly. You want people who can get work done on their own, and who are also good at tackling a project as a team, dividing the work, and sharing the results because they're accountable to each other and to the team. These components all build an engaged culture.

As I discussed in the last section, having an engaged culture in the workplace is correlated with financial success for that company. Now I grant that correlation isn't the same as causation, so maybe you can have an engaged team, but still not have a great company. But given a choice between a team of hard-working, highly engaged and collaborating people at a second rate company, and a group (let's not even call it a team) of self-centered, back-stabbing people at a Fortune 500 company, I know which one I'd rather work on.

5 / MAKING PEOPLE YOUR MOST IMPORTANT ASSET

The most important thing is to try and inspire people so that they can be great in whatever they want to do.
–Kobe Bryant

The first component of the culture equation is People. As I discussed in the last chapter, demographic and technological shifts will be impacting our world, making it harder to find people with the right skills, and who are available to do the work. Here in the world of accounting, the talent crunch is only going to get worse. As of the end of the third quarter of 2019, the unemployment rate for financial managers was 1.8%.[1] And according to a Robert Half report, 93% of accounting and finance leaders surveyed in the fall of 2018 reported having a hard time finding the right people.[2]

The talent crunch in accounting isn't new. Since at least 2015, the Journal of Accountancy has been running articles noting that the inflow of new talent at CPA firms isn't keeping up with the outflows due to Baby Boomer retirement and attrition.[3] The struggle to find talent spreads across industry: 85% of the accountants we surveyed in 2018[4] reported having a hard time attracting and retaining talent.

Solving this challenge means taking a multi-pronged approach. Developing the people on your team is the best way to get the skills you need. But before you develop people, you need to get the right people on your team, so I'll also look at how you hire and retain people. Building the accounting team of the future means your team needs more than just knowledge of debits, credits, and GAAP. So I'll also talk about the other skills your team will need.

Let's look at these pieces of the solution...

MAKE PEOPLE YOUR COMPANY'S MOST VALUABLE ASSET

To make sure you really do make the most out of your people, you've got to understand how to meet their needs, and how they can best contribute to your team. So let's first take a look at the generational changes that we know are happening.

"Talking 'bout my generation..."

When Roger Daltrey of The Who belted that out back in 1967, way before I was born, he was talking about the Baby

Boomers who were rebelling against parents who had lived through World War II, the Korean War, and maybe even the Great Depression.

Today, everyone seems to be dumping on the Millennial generation. We're self-centered, lazy, and lack ambition. Too many of us still live with our parents. We're impatient. We don't want to pay our dues. We want instant gratification, and don't want to wait around for promotions up the corporate ladder.

The truth is, we only seem that way because we've been given the gift of technology to do our jobs — and we know how to use it. Instead of spending hours doing something manually, we'll find an app to do it for us in seconds.

That technology has given us access to knowledge and insights that previous generations didn't have. This transparency makes Trust and Accountability, the other two parts of our Culture equation, mandatory. We're not afraid to call bullshit on others.

So let's take a look at what these generational differences mean in our People element.

Today, five generations are working side by side, though there aren't many of the oldest generation still in the workplace:

- Greatest Generation (born 1922-1943)
- Baby Boomers (born 1943-1960)
- Generation X (born 1960-1980)
- Generation Y or Millennials (born 1980-1995)
- Generation Z (born 1995 - 2012)

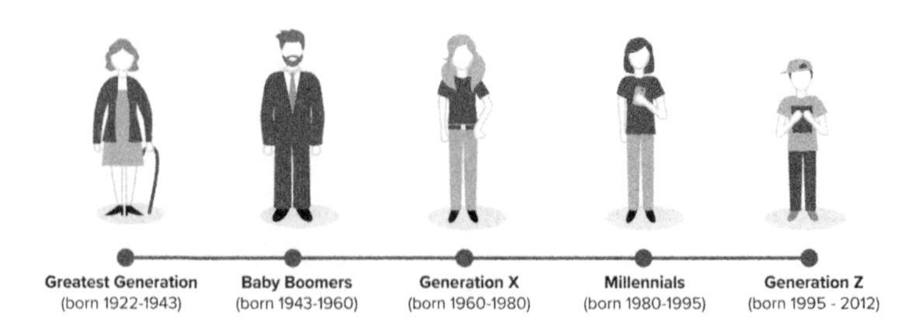

Much has been made about the differences between the ways these generations approach work and life. For example, Greatest Generation members are loyal, and believe in paying their dues, so they may be more likely to stick it out in a job for their entire career, even if it's one they hate. Baby Boomers value personal growth and are ambitious. They tend to have more loyalty to their careers than to a specific employer. Gen Xers value diversity and work/life balance, and don't take kindly to micromanaging. Millennials are comfortable with change, so they may be more likely to job hop than other generations. Gen Z, whose members are just now entering the workforce, are competitive, independent, and are likely to have a side hustle.

However, according to a few academic studies cited in an article on The Balance,[5] these differences may have more to do with someone's current career stage. For example, someone who is nearing retirement age may be loyal to that employer because they just want to hang on for a few more years. But someone who has just entered the workforce may skip around between jobs until they figure out what they want to do.

Nevertheless, it is true that as cultures across the world morph and change, the cultural norms that we were raised in leave a mark on us. What is clear is that Millennials, like every generation before them, are changing the culture of the workplace.

And by 2025, as much as 75% of the workforce will be Millennials.

Though academic surveys of the workplace found no real generational differences, surveys of consumer attitudes towards businesses as reported by the Brookings Institution[6] have shown clear generational differences. Between 2005 and 2009, just as the first Millennials reached adulthood, attributes favored by Gen X, such as *exclusive*, *arrogant*, and *sensuous* were displaced in favor of *kindness* and *empathy*. Those latter two attributes rose 391% over that five year period.

Yep, that's right. Millennials, who are supposedly self-centered narcissists, highly value kindness and empathy, which are both kind of incompatible with being self-centered.

The authors of the Brookings Institution report point out that Millennial consumers make purchasing decisions based on affinity with the values of a corporation. A company's public stance and actions regarding social issues encourage like-minded Millennials to purchase from that company, even at a higher price. Companies seeking scarce talent should pay attention to this, because "the strategy that must be employed to win Millennial consumers' loyalty, is the same one that must be used to win the loyalty of the company's Millennial employees."[7]

These ideas are echoed in Deloitte's 2018 survey[8] of Millennials and Generation Z members around the globe. Deloitte found that young employees have greater loyalty to organizations that demonstrate these attributes:

- **Flexibility in work hours and locations** — 55% of Millennials who expect to stay with their current employer for more than five years said they have greater flexibility now than three years ago.
- **Compensation** — 63% of Millennials and 51% of

Gen Zers cite pay as a factor in deciding to work for an organization.

- **Positive workplace culture** — Younger workers believe companies should operate to create jobs and innovative products, benefit society overall, and not solely to generate profits.
- **Diversity** — Millennials and Gen Zers broaden the definition of diversity beyond the obvious demographic factors like age, culture, and economic status to encompass differences, tolerance, inclusion, and openness to new ideas. Diversity also includes diversity in the kinds of colleges and universities people attend.
- **Continuing training and education** — Younger workers say that only about one-quarter of the skills and knowledge they need for their jobs came from their college education. They expect businesses to fill in the gaps, and especially for the continuing digital transformation.

WHAT DOES THIS MEAN FOR CONTROLLERS?

Millennials seek out work that has meaning, and want to be happier at work than our parents. We may be more motivated by personal growth than by a fat paycheck. Prompt feedback from a trusted mentor is more useful than an annual performance review. Tools that enable collaboration and accountability will help us do our best.

Gen Z, on the other hand, witnessed the struggles of their parents and neighbors during the financial crisis, and may be looking for a steady paycheck and a clear path for advancement. Their independence and competitive spirit can be nurtured by gamifying training or creating in-house contests. Remember that this generation has never been without wifi and smartphones, so they'll expect a connected tech environment.

Here's what my co-founder Chris Sluty says about younger generations in the workplace:

> *For those of us in the younger generations, we look to technology to solve our problems. And we're certainly more open to it because it's what we know. I've got people on my team that have never lived without the internet. It's just a whole different way of thinking than somebody who grew up without it. So hopefully, as these younger generations start becoming part of management, they're really looking for tools for operational efficiency.*

And while much has been made of the demands that Millennials and Gen Z make on employers, the truth is that what we vociferously and confidently demand are the same things that everyone has always wanted, but has been afraid to ask for: flexibility, continuous professional and personal development, a clear career path upward, and meaningful work.

Demographics and an acute shortage of accountants are on the side of younger generations. If we don't get what we want from your company, finding a new job is just a few mouse clicks away.

Review Note: Maybe the solution isn't more employees

If you've got a special project malingering on the back burner, consider hiring outside contractors to get it done. Thanks to the internet, it's easier than you might think to hire temporary workers on a project basis. The same forces that are making it possible for remote work are also encouraging skilled professionals to operate as contractors or independent consultants.

Despite popular opinion, many of these temporary contract basis workers are not young kids straight out of college, trying to finance their world travels.

According to Marion McGovern, author of *Thriving in the Gig Economy*,[9] many contract workers come from the Baby Boomer generation. These may be highly experienced accountants who aren't quite ready to trade in their ten-keys for golf clubs, or who need to keep working for financial reasons.

While these older contract workers may not be as tech savvy as the younger ones, they do have decades of business insight and experience.

Those contract workers might also be Millennials with several years of experience. According to the Deloitte Millennial survey,[10] seven in ten Millennials in senior management positions would consider short-term contract work as an alternative to full-time jobs and as a way to make more money.

Here are a few places you might look:

Robert Half

AccountingFly

MCW

HOW TO RECRUIT, HIRE, AND (MOST IMPORTANTLY) RETAIN

Southwest Airlines has been profitable for 47 consecutive years. A key to that was the culture that founder Herb Kelleher created. He proved it was possible to create a profitable company that cared about employees as if they were family. In hiring, Herb looked for attitude, not skills. As he famously said, "You don't hire for skills, you hire for attitude. You can always teach skills." But Southwest Airlines isn't an anomaly. Hiring the right people has been the secret to success for many great companies.

GETTING THE RIGHT PEOPLE ON YOUR BUS

Nearly 20 years ago, Jim Collins spent several years researching publicly traded companies that had made the leap from merely good to great, and that had sustained that greatness, as measured by stock prices, for at least 20 years. As he documented in his book *From Good to Great,* one of the commonalities for the companies that made the leap was that they first got the right people on the bus, the wrong people off the bus, and the right people in the right seats on the bus.

> The good-to-great leaders understood three simple truths. First, if you begin with "who," rather than "what," you can more easily adapt to a changing world… Second, if you have the right people on the bus, the problem of how to motivate and manage people largely goes away. The right people don't need to be tightly managed or fired up; they will be self-motivated by the inner drive to produce the best results and to be part of creating something great. Third, if you have the wrong people, it doesn't matter whether you discover the right direction; you still won't have a great company. Great vision without great people is irrelevant.

11

For example, as Collins describes in the book, when Nucor began experimenting with mini-mills to take on giant Bethlehem Steel, CEO Ken Iverson built "its entire system on the idea that you can teach farmers how to make steel, but you can't teach a farmer work ethic to people who don't have it in the first place."[12] So he built a network of small steel mills in rural areas, not in the traditional manufacturing centers, and hired farmers to work in them. These farmers had an incredible work ethic: "'Gotta milk the cows' and 'Gonna plow the north forty before noon' translated easily into 'Gotta roll some sheet steel' and 'Gonna cast forty tons before lunch.'"

HOW WE HIRE AT FLOQAST

With Derek Mernagh's recommendation to build a strong team in mind, hiring is something I recommend that controllers spend a good deal of time on. The philosophy I have had since day one is that you want to hire people to take work off your plate. So, the requirement I have for anyone I hire is that they have to be better than me at the job.

I've always looked for someone who can tell me what to do and give me advice. That mentality takes a lot of confidence and the ability to swallow your pride. You have to have the confidence that none of these people are going to take my job. They're here to help make my team better and make our company better, which is ultimately going to make me look like the best manager out there.

As accountants, we're in the knowledge business. Accounting requires a high level of knowledge. And the lack of knowledge out there is starting to make hiring more difficult, which was confirmed by the 85% of accountants[13] in our survey who said that it was hard to find and keep the right people.

So you have to be much more specific about who you're targeting, and you need to have high standards. If that hire isn't the right one, it's a big hit to the company. It can set you back several months, or even quarters, depending on the seniority of that position.

We very closely follow a scorecard hiring methodology referred to as the Who hiring method. This comes from a book by Geoff Smart and Randy People called *Who: The A*

Method for Hiring. This book focuses on finding the right talent for the C-suite and top level management, but we've found it useful at every level.

The first step is to sit down as a team and really collaborate and come up with a job description. But it's not just a job description — it's coming up with the skills that you're looking for, the competencies that they need to have, and then the results that you want to see from this person.

And then you interview in a very specific way. You go through that scorecard and check off the items. Ultimately you give each candidate a score. This method allows you to be very objective about the interview process. You really consider the candidate's traits, background, and skills, more than going with a gut reaction. You can be far more critical and way more objective about it with this methodology.

Sourcing your candidates is another important part of this process. If you only rely on ads or help from recruiters when you need someone, you'll have a hard time finding the right candidates, especially for the higher positions.

Instead, you need to develop your own pool of candidates.

The best way to do this is to reach out to your network for referrals and ask everyone you know this simple question: "Who are the most talented people you know who could be a good fit for my company?" Ask your employees for referrals also. As you get names, contact these people every now and then to get to know them. Then when you do need someone, you've got a pool of excellent candidates.

I love this hiring method. It's made us significantly more effective. I've definitely seen a material impact on all of our hiring. Our success rate has gone up dramatically.

. . .

Review Note: Hiring right means less micro-managing

Our Director of Human Resources, Adey Tadesse-Heath, says that by attracting "like-attitude" people, we're getting something we wouldn't get if we just looked for technical rockstars:

> *We like to hire people who are smarter than us. That way they can go ahead and do the job better than I ever would. I don't have to micromanage the people on my team, because they are proactive. They'll find projects to work on and I just tell them to check in with me when they need something.*
>
> *Now I have free time because I'm not doing that project. I can do something else. I have a feeling that a lot of those hiring managers feel the same way. So we've learned to zero in on people who give you the sense that they can come in here and just hit the ground running and be autonomous.*

MCW

THE MOST IMPORTANT SKILLS FOR THE FUTURE

I always look for attitude and a desire for learning and improvement. Cultural fit is more important than skills, which can be taught. But besides attitude, here are some skills besides a firm understanding of debits, credits, and GAAP that finance teams of the future will need.

Data analytics

As accountants, we've always analyzed data and offered insights, but with cloud technology, we now have access to more data than ever before. And thanks to automation, we're no longer compiling that data. When we marry that financial data with non-financial data, and turn it into insights for other parts of the organization, magic happens.

Some companies go further, and hire specialists with advanced degrees in data analysis and data science (see Review Note) to do this heavy-duty number crunching, data visualization, and coding.

Fortunately, the AICPA is is now offering a five-part, 63-hour certificate program in data analytics,[14] and on a smaller budget, Udemy even has low-cost courses in data analysis and data science.[15] Many universities are also offering courses in data analysis as part of their accounting curriculum.

Tech agility

If you're hiring digital natives, this won't be much of a problem for a generation that didn't need to be taught how to FaceTime. They simply did it. However, some of these younger folks have never used a PC, so they may need basic instruction in how to work with one. But for Gen X and older team members, tech agility can be an issue. Maybe it's because the earliest DOS-based computers were so hard to use, they developed an unconscious aversion to technology. Today, the ability to use different pieces of technology is as essential as using a 10-key was in my days at EY.

But more important than tech agility is the ability and the desire to learn new skills. Whatever tech we're using today will be different in a few years. Today's accountants need to be willing to learn new tools as they come on the market, and to experiment with connecting them and building platforms that let you automate as much as possible.

Communication skills

An old stereotype of an accountant is someone who sits in a back office with a green eye shade and an adding machine and is more interested in numbers than people. But as controllers take on a more strategic role in their companies, the ability to communicate financial and numeric data to non-accountants is crucial. Verbal, written, and presentation skills are essential today.

A great resource for finance professionals who want to improve their presentation skills is the book *Taking the Numb Out of Numbers* by Peter Margaritis, CPA. Peter applies the principles of improv and storytelling to communicating complex financial information so that the audience understands and remembers what you were trying to communicate. Hint: No giant Excel spreadsheets in 10 point font in your PowerPoint slides.

Another great option is joining Toastmasters, which I did to improve my public speaking skills (more about that later).

Creative problem solving

If you're reading this book, you know that the problems faced by accounting and business today require more than the solutions that worked in the past. And you've probably found that using the analytic side of your brain to look at a problem from different points of view somehow lights up the creative side to solve a problem by connecting the dots, as described in an AICPA interview with a Google executive.[16] Fortunately, creative problem solving can be taught.

Here are some ideas to get you started:

1. **Start by asking better questions.** Peter Block's thought-provoking book, *The Answer to How is Yes,* suggests that when we ask questions with "how," we may be limiting our options to what others before us have done, instead of seeking to do work that really matters. For example, he recommends that instead of asking "How have others done something similar?" we should ask "What do we want to create together?"

Instead of asking "How much does it cost?" we should ask "What is the price I am willing to pay?"

2. **Change perspective.** Take off your controller hat, and consider how someone in marketing might view the issue. Or talk the problem out, as if you were explaining it to a six-year-old or your (non-accountant) great-aunt.
3. **Get out of the office and do something completely different.** In his book, *Where Good Ideas Come From,* Steven Johnson tells the story of how a Parisian obstetrician in the 1870s got the idea of neonatal incubators from a trip to the Paris Zoo, where he saw an exhibit of chicken incubators.
4. **Take a lesson from improv.** One of the foundational elements of improv is to always respond with "Yes! And…" instead of "No, because…" Responding with "No, because" puts a block in front of the idea as a possible solution. But when you respond with "Yes, and" that leaves the idea open to further development and expansion.
5. **Begin with the end in mind.** This is habit #2 of Stephen Covey's *The 7 Habits of Highly Successful People.* Instead of focusing on the challenges facing you, think about the end outcome you want to achieve.

A more formulaic approach comes from Alex Osborn and Sid Parmes' Creative Problem Solving framework,[17] which they began developing in the 1940s. Their iterative four-step process is as follows:

- **Clarify**: Identify the challenge or goal, gather information, and formulate challenge questions that rephrase the challenge or goal as questions.

- **Ideate**: Generate ideas that answer the challenge questions.
- **Develop**: Formulate solutions by evaluating the generated ideas to come up with the best fit.
- **Implement**: Create a plan to implement the selected solution.

The exact process you use to juice up your creative problem solving skills matters less than being willing to work those brain cells to make new connections between ideas.

LEARN FROM THE OLDER GENERATION BEFORE THEY ALL WALK OUT THE DOOR

This might not be much of an issue for young startups, but companies that have been around for a few decades are facing the potential loss of proprietary knowledge, business insights, and wisdom when long-time Baby Boomer executives and senior managers retire. Some younger team members who want to change the world of business may think this isn't a bad thing. But before those people leave, try to capture their wisdom before they leave by recording video interviews, or ask them to stay on as consultants and demonstrate by example what they do as a matter of instinct.

One thing I'm noticing is that younger managers are not as good at communicating with their teams, particularly when they're having tough conversations. I think that you can read all you want about communication and how to deliver messages, and you can watch YouTube videos all day, but you have to have worked with and managed different types of people and different personalities and different situations to really know how to navigate those variables.

For example, our Vice President of Sales, Jill Cooper, has been working with sales reps for 30 years, so she's 10 chess moves ahead of them because she's had these conversations dozens of times. Recently, we raised the quotas on our account executives, so they were all pissed off.

So Jill went to the sales rep who was the most fired up about the change, and flipped the conversation. By the end, he agreed with the increase, and even said maybe the sales quotas should have been increased more. Here's how that conversation went:

"You know, we've done all these things to empower you as a salesperson. We've put out more products to support you with more leads. We're investing more heavily in you. So we expect you to be able to return more to us internally.

"Conversely, let's say we didn't deliver on these products that we promised and we had kept your sales quotas in place. If we didn't deliver the products, do you think it would be fair for you to request a reduced quota?" When the sales rep said yes, she asked him, "So why isn't that a two way street?"

I genuinely believe you have to hear the actual talk track and see a demonstration of someone having those difficult conversations. Now that I've heard the story, it's in my tool bag and I can use it forever.

At Cornerstone, I was lucky to have my desk outside the CFO's office, and he kept his door open when he made calls. So I got to hear him all the time and learned by osmosis from him.

Younger accountants and controllers can take active measures to gain from people in positions you aspire to. Ask to be involved in the kinds of situations you want to learn about. This is something you can't learn on YouTube or from textbooks.

. . .

Review Note: Data analytics and data science

Data analytics and data science are two of the most in-demand skills for the future. Data analysts examine large sets of data for trends, and create visualizations to help businesses make decisions. Data scientists take that analysis a step further by developing algorithms to test predictions. Both have training in statistics, data visualization, and may be fluent in multiple programming languages. By one definition, "a data scientist is someone who knows more programming than a statistician, and more statistics than a software engineer."[18]

Many universities around the country are offering undergraduate and graduate programs in data analytics and data science. This means it's conceivable that someone on your team could pick up these advanced skills on the side, but more likely, if your organization grows to the point of needing one, you'll hire one from outside.

Demand is outpacing supply for these skills, so if you hire a data analyst or data scientist, you can expect this to be pricey. Because the demand is so high, and because many companies are still learning what data analysts and scientists do, these people tend to do a lot of job hopping.

Even if you don't learn to code or take a deep dive into statistics, as a finance leader, you'll have to learn enough about data science to interface with any experts your company hires. Developing a data strategy and an understanding of the work that data scientists and data analysts perform before you bring one on board will help ward off the frustration that causes high turnover in these positions, as data scientist Jonny Brooks-Bartlett describes in an article aptly titled "Here's why so many data scientists are leaving their jobs."[19]

Many companies bring on a data scientist with the belief that hiring one will solve all their data problems, but "many companies hire data scientists without a suitable infrastructure in place to start getting value out of AI," according to Brooks-Bartlett. So make sure that you have the infrastructure in place, as Monica Rogatti describes in a blog post on Hackernoon.[20]

Rogatti puts AI at the top of a "pyramid of needs." Before you can really leverage AI, you've got to have the supporting infrastructure in place. Your organization needs to be able to collect the data it needs, move that data through the system, and explore the data to ensure it's complete and reliable. At that point, you can start to analyze and employ simple machine learning to perform simple tests. Finally, when you have all of that infrastructure in place, you can really maximize on the potential of AI.

CREATIVE WAYS TO FIND TALENT

Millennials and Gen Zers estimate that only about a quarter of the skills and knowledge they need for their jobs came from their college degree.[21] The rest came from on-the-job training. This confirms that the best candidates for a job are the ones with a hunger, a desire to learn more.

Consider broadening the talent pool by looking in places the competition isn't. Accounting firms in Australia and the UK hire kids right out of high school to work part time as apprentices while they earn an accounting degree.

Maybe the talent you need is right under your nose. One of my friends told me about a receptionist with a degree in communications her CPA firm hired. That young woman proved to be a whiz at taxes, and is now working on an accounting degree while she works full-time in the tax department.

In an article in the Journal of Accountancy,[22] Kathy Lockhart, VP of finance and controller for Noodles & Co, talks about training former data entry clerks for higher level finance jobs. So maybe there's someone in operations or marketing who would make a great accountant. But you won't know that if you're not out there, talking to people across your organization.

The best way I've found to source quality candidates is from referral sources, as I mentioned above, using the Who method.[23] Ask everyone you know, everyone you meet, other controllers, and your employees "Who are the most talented people you know who could be a good fit for my company?" Put those names on a list, and reach out to them periodically.

WHAT TO DO AFTER YOU HIRE

When you onboard an employee in accounting, I'm very much a fan of giving them an overview of the whole process. But what usually happens is that a manager will just plug the new hire directly into the specific process that they'll be working on. When you do that, the new employee doesn't have a sense of the bigger picture, and they're not really as bought in to their role. They don't understand how their work is going to impact others in accounting and the business as a whole.

So show them the landscape. A good way to do that is to have them sit down with each of your team members and learn a little bit about what each of those people do so they can start to understand their role in the context of the whole department.

Another way is to give them a copy of the balance sheet or the trial balance. Have them work down the list of accounts and learn how each of those accounts work. Then give them their task or specific role. Now that they understand why each account is important, they should understand how their work impacts other people on their team, and the company at large as well.

Once the new hire is settled in their job, you need a method to monitor their work. One thing that's difficult in accounting is understanding who your top performers are. I've found the key is tracking three things about how they're doing their job:

1. How accurate is their work?
2. Are they a hard worker?
3. Are they a team player?

It's not hard to monitor whether the work is being done correctly or not. But it can be hard to interpret who's taking on the most work and who's taking it easy. The last one is the most important, and the best way to do that is to understand their workload.

However, unless you have a tool to monitor that workload, transparency and accountability is a challenge. An ideal tool lets controllers monitor who's who's taking on the most work and who's creating a bottleneck. This elevates the top performers and identifies them so that you can reward them. On the flip side, this also identifies the bottlenecks, process inefficiencies, and low performers.

When you shine a spotlight on the low performers, I find that one of two things happen. One, you get an increase in productivity because they're aware of that spotlight on them. Or, two, they end up leaving the organization. If number two happens, congratulations! Now you have the opportunity to backfill your team with a high performer.

Transparency and accountability puts everyone's work front and center, enabling you to build a high performing team. When you put great software together with great people, that's how you get great results.

What you don't want is one person who's overworked, staying late at the office until 10 o'clock every night with other team members only working until five. That doesn't create a good team dynamic.

A better dynamic is when that person who's done early goes to the team member who's always working late and asks, "Can I help you with any of this work? What can I take off your plate?"

That's the culture you need. You don't want people working as individuals and siloed off. You can only get this by building transparency and accountability into your culture.

So I'm always asking my managers to report back on who's the team player, and who just wants to get their job done. That's a really great way to stay on top of it. The unfortunate reality is that people are either team players or they're not. Once you do identify someone who's not being a team player, it's probably in the best interest to move on from them as quickly as possible.

HOW TO KEEP PEOPLE

The best way to retain people is to hire the right ones to begin with. A good cultural fit in a company that matches their values, a feeling of being appreciated along with the right pay and benefits, will keep your team loyal.

One key thing that really makes a difference in keeping people around is having good managers. When people have bosses they actually want to work for and enjoy working for, that makes a big difference.

Salary, remote work, flexible schedules, and benefits will only get you so far. These are table stakes in today's tight job market. Millennial and Gen Z employees expect it, and many of your older employees will appreciate it. According to Deloitte's latest Millennial survey,[24] the top three things Millennials and Gen Zers look for in a new employer are pay and benefits, a positive workplace culture, and flexibility.

To keep employees around, a diverse work culture helps. That same survey said that although younger workers don't seem to seek out employers with a diverse workforce, 69% of Millennials who plan on staying in their job for five years or more say that they work in a diverse organization.

These younger team members don't define diversity strictly along demographic lines. For them, diversity encompasses inclusivity, tolerance, respect, and different ways of thinking, as well as different ages, cultures, lifestyles, and a variety of educational backgrounds.

ENGAGED PEOPLE STAY LONGER

According to Gallup's most recent meta-analysis of employee engagement,[25] engaged employees are more likely to stay longer. Gallup found that within organizations with a low overall turnover rate, the highly engaged business units within those organizations had an employee turnover rate that was 59% lower than average.

Also, as I mentioned in the last chapter, engagement isn't about making your employees happy. It's about challenging them and giving them the tools for success. Those tools include tech solutions that take away error-prone boring work. Besides being deadly dull, it's hard to be excited about work when your day consists of racing through manual processes that require focus, but don't let you exercise the higher parts of your intellect.

Engagement is about connecting their values to the Why of the finance team and the Why of the whole organization. As Grant and Notter say in their book, *The Non-Obvious Guide to Employee Engagement*, "Engagement is a result of a crisp alignment between individual success and organizational success."

My CEO at Cornerstone was great about this. He was always talking about the company's overall strategy and where we were going. If you were paying attention, you could understand how you fit into that machine and how you were going to help impact it.

For me, understanding where we were going as a company on

a high level was really motivating and engaging. It wasn't just "I'm going to my desk and doing the work and going home, and the next day is going to be like today."

Knowing the Why behind what we were doing, I could see we were part of an awesome growth company, and I could see the impact of what I was doing. I could also see that I wasn't going to do the same thing in 12 months as what I'm doing today. So even if it was momentarily boring, I could see that I was part of something bigger than myself.

MILLENNIALS NEED TO UNDERSTAND WHY

To really engage your Millennial team members, you have to take them through the Golden Circle of Why, How and What. Understanding the Golden Circle is something I've found to be really key for managing Millennials. They won't be too interested if you just show them what to do without explaining why they're doing the work. When they understand the Why of the organization, and the Why of the accounting department, and if they really resonate with it, they'll come up with creative ways to figure out the How and What.

As an example, at FloQast, one of our big initiatives is NetSuite First. That's because we've historically done really well with NetSuite users, largely because FloQast is more efficient with NetSuite than with other ERPs. So I put this out to the company as an initiative for us to focus on because that's what's important for us to succeed as a business.

What's been interesting is watching how that all cascades down and seeing how people run with that big goal. So different team members have been coming up with creative ways to identify more NetSuite accounts we can go after. For example, the marketing folks created super targeted marketing initiatives. So I'm not necessarily directing how or what people are doing, but just letting them go to their strengths, and empowering them to implement these new things.

They wouldn't be doing any of this, though, if they didn't resonate with the big Why of FloQast: to help accountants close the books faster and more accurately, and to create a better life at work for accountants.

It's not only Millennials who benefit from having a big Why to rally around that engages them to work hard and take inspired action. It's just that this generation has a bigger view of the world, and of life in general, than just a 9 to 5 job with a paycheck that lets them buy the house and the car and raise a family. I really think that everyone in the workplace, whatever generation they're in, lives up to their full potential and capitalizes on their strengths when they're inspired by an organization that has a big Why.

TRAIN THEM SO WELL THEY CAN GO ANYWHERE, BUT TREAT THEM SO WELL THEY'LL STAY FOREVER

According to Deloitte's Millennial Survey, Millennials and Gen Z employees say that only about a quarter of the skills, knowledge, and experience they need to do their job came from their university studies.[26] For older workers, who are further from their college days, this is even smaller. And with the rapid fire changes from FASB for revenue recognition and lease accounting, not to mention the ever-changing technology we use every day, even less of what controllers and finance teams need to know came from accounting classes or CPA exam prep courses.

This means that workplaces have to pick up the slack. Investing in team members isn't cheap. Looking at the costs of getting everyone up to speed, many controllers and CFOs wonder about the wisdom of that investment if those employees leave in just a couple of years. But consider what it would be like if you don't make that investment to teach your employees new skills and they stay forever.

Of course, there's no blanket rule for teaching people. There are some roles in a company where you teach them how to do one thing, and the person in that role is content to do that for years. They come in, do their job, and go home to their family. That's great, and you need people like that on your team.

But for the people who want to learn new skills, you've got to support that. Supporting your people means not just understanding what they need to learn to do their jobs now, but also understanding what they'll need in the future. I like this story about Jac Emeril, controller at Blue Cross Blue Shield of Michigan, from a report by the AICPA and CIMA.[27] Jac had his finance team learn Six Sigma, robotics, and AI, and said:

> I challenged people: learn the new skill, practice the new skill, pick somewhere you're spending significant time and energy and build yourself a bot. Who can save the most time in their daily jobs?

Encourage your team members to "punch above their weight class." This stretches people, and stretching people in a good way makes them more engaged. To succeed, they have no choice but to pick up the knowledge and skills they need. Employers who help their team members by helping them to learn what they need to become successful will have engaged, smart, and valuable folks on their team.

REGULAR RECOGNITION PAYS BIG DIVIDENDS

Don't forget about the importance of regular recognition. If your team members feel neglected or that their work isn't noticed, they might be inclined to seek greener pastures where their talents are appreciated. Here at FloQast, we recognize our team members' hard work at several levels, as Adey Tadesse-Heath, Director of Human Resources, explains:

> *At the company level, we have two methods for recognition. First, we have a #gratitude channel in Slack. All employees belong to it, and any employee can drop a #gratitude. So for example, '#gratitude to Kat for going out of her way to help me on a project that she wasn't responsible for in any way.' This way I get to showcase my appreciation for her hard work and give it visibility when no one else might have seen it before.*
>
> *So anyone can drop some gratitude, and it might seem small to just make a comment, but it lets others see that there are team members who are helping people from different departments when they didn't have to. It also lets people see a little bit more of how the departments interact.*
>
> *The second method we have is quarterly company-wide recognition. Each quarter, the VPs and the C suite will pick three people to receive a gratitude award. Mike, the CEO, announces it in our all-company meeting with a little blurb about why they these people were chosen.*
>
> *You don't get awards for just doing your job, you get an award for going above and beyond. The winners get to choose a cash bonus or a fully vested stock option grant.*
>
> *I've heard really good feedback from some of the winners. They mostly don't expect to win. It also helps everyone understand what different people in the company do and how it impacts the business and the success of the company.*

You might notice that some of the methods we use for recognition don't cost anything. To be impactful, the cost of the method is less important than just doing it. Little things like a birthday cake or a #gratitude comment in Slack convey to your team that you're not taking them for granted.

Review Note: A word about compensation

Oftentimes people do leave over compensation. There's not much you can do for someone if that's their main motivation. Back at EY, we would get inflation raises, but we were still always undercompensated by 20 to 30% relative to what you could get in a new job. People who went the industry route could get even more. So at EY, they were always emphasizing the learning opportunity and how much more money you would make the longer you waited to go into private. Plus, there was the CPA exam and your CPA license up for stake. But that strategy doesn't work when that's not what's on the line.

At FloQast, we give proactive raises to fair market value, not inflation adjustments. We'll do salary band exercises where we'll take a look at the fair market value salary for a given position. Then within that band range, we'll compensate people based on how much experience they have for that job.

If you're transparent and you're telling people that you're leveling them up and you're giving them a raise to fair market value, that's much less of a reason to want to look for another job.

It's in the best interest of the business to keep your best people in the constant extra 10% over market value, rather than having them turnover. Replacing them is usually more expensive than that 10% extra. Plus, there's all the knowledge that you lose with them, so it's a pretty easy argument to be made.

MCW

EMPOWER YOUR TEAM

Most accountants in industry got their start in public accounting, which tends to be a very top-down, SALY mentality.

Doing anything differently or adding a new tech tool means wading through layers of managers and partners to get approval. And mostly the answer is no. Creativity is actively discouraged. We do it this way because that's the way we do it. That kind of rigid mentality means that those who like to think and learn often leave accounting altogether.

But there are a few accountants out there who embrace innovation and want to empower their team members. We've got one of those here in the form of CPO Chris Sluty, who was fortunate to have worked under an audit partner who questioned the status quo:

> *When I moved out to California, for the first time ever, I had a partner that questioned the company's processes. We had our audit programs and he would say to us, "But why are we doing it that way?" And we'd answer, "Well, that's the way we do it." That was never good enough for him. That had a profound effect on me because it really changed my mindset.*
>
> *And what I took away from that experience is if you give people opportunities to own things that they're passionate about, but maybe their title doesn't say they should be running point on this project, then they're going to really, really care because they're making changes here. They're the boots on the ground. They're the most intimate with our internal process. They know how to fix things. If somebody's going to execute on a vision, they've got to be bought in on it. So I think the big thing for us is giving people opportunities. Mike uses the term "punch above their weight class."*

How does Chris' approach impact people on his team? One of his team members, Troy Patipanavat, spent two years in public accounting under micromanaging seniors, managers, and partners who would regularly shoot down ideas to make things more efficient. So he was shocked when Chris gave him a level of autonomy and empowerment that made him feel like he was his own boss:

> *The fact that Chris allowed me to make my own decisions meant that he truly believed in me, and this propelled me to work harder because I was managing projects from start to end on my own. When Chris allowed me to fully manage a process, it provided a new challenge for me. That empowerment gave me freedom of expression when making decisions. It allowed me to step up to the plate to meet the challenge.*
>
> *I've grown immensely through this type of leadership style, which allows me to impact the company overall in its greater vision.*
>
> *Trust is not given, it's earned. I didn't arrive at this level of autonomy in one week. It was a process of building trust with my team over a period of time.*
>
> *So when I come to Chris and say, "Here are my two options. Should I do A or B?" Chris says "Troy, do what you think is best." I have the freedom to fail and learn from that. I'm more invested. It's my own project.*

A big part of empowerment is making sure everyone is clear on the What-How-Why Golden Circle that Simon Sinek talks about. When your team is clear on the Why of what you're doing, then you can trust them to make the How decisions that lead to the What results.

An environment where accountants feel empowered and trusted to make the right decisions is unfortunately still rare. It's rare enough that if you can create that, and find team players who buy into your Why, then give them ownership over a project they care about, they'll stay a lot longer than if they just feel like a cog in a big machine.

CREATIVE WAYS TO HELP YOUR TEAM LEARN

Traditionally, businesses have simply hired new employees and laid off the old ones when they need a team with new skills. This is partly because most companies aren't very good at assessing the skills of their current employees, and by the time they figure that out, it's too late. With the ongoing and projected talent crunch in accounting, that doesn't work too well. The people with the accounting and technology skills that accounting departments need aren't there.

A recent article in the Wall Street Journal demonstrates the ways that workers whose jobs are at risk of disappearing can apply their current skill sets to jobs of the future.[28] For example, a data-entry clerk could develop their detail-oriented skills in combination with additional education and training to become an e-commerce analyst, loan officer or customer success manager.

As explained in the McKinsey report, *Skill Shift*, retraining staff involves three distinct actions:[29]

1. **Teaching current staff skills that are qualitatively different from what they already do.** For example, teaching an accounts payable clerk to prepare reports or basic analysis for the sales team.
2. **Improving and updating the skills of current staff to keep up with changes in technology.** This includes teaching members of the accounting team to use the new accounting tech stack you're deploying.
3. **Hiring entry level workers with the goal of training them in the skills they need.** This could be helping that accounts payable clerk get an accounting degree.

Online courses

YouTube and Udemy are the big names. Massive Open Online Course (MOOC) platforms like Coursera offer, for example, an IBM Data Science Professional Certificate, along with hundreds of accounting courses taught by major universities around the world. EdX, founded by Harvard and MIT, also has hundreds of courses in accounting and finance, data science, and management.

Webinars from software providers

Don't overlook these as a free (but maybe biased) source of helping your team learn new skills. At FloQast, we do a ton of these, not only to let people know what FloQast does, but also to help current users know what else we can help them with.

Vendor conferences

Conferences like Sage Intacct Advantage and Oracle Netsuite SuiteWorld put you and your team in a venue with thousands of other users, who are also looking for better ways to do their work. Besides going to sessions to hear about best practices, you can also meet other controllers going through the same challenges you are. Then there are the vendors, who will be more than happy to explain what their solution can do for you.

Review Note: Hybrid skills are what's needed in the future

As technology takes over more of the number-crunching, to remain relevant, accountants will need to pick up the creative skills that computers can't handle. A recent article in the Wall Street Journal[30] described the hybrid jobs of the future as "... positions, which require skills not normally found together. For example, these hybrid jobs might require people with skills in data science and advertising, or engineering and sales."

For accountants, a hot combination is accounting and IT, according to an article by Robert Half senior executive director Paul McDonald.[31] But other valuable combinations might be accounting plus communication, or accounting plus operations. Or maybe all of the above. At any rate, accounting in the future will be less focused on tasks, and will require more creativity than in the past.

GIVE YOUR PEOPLE A CLEAR PATH FORWARD

One thing that all generations have in common is an aversion to being stuck in a dead-end position. You don't want your best people to think they're in a dark tunnel with no way out. It really helps people to know what they need to do to get to the next level.

Accounting and finance are especially notorious in this respect. Someone might have five years of experience, but it's really the same year of experience, repeated five times. You don't want your people to feel like that.

Accountants are naturally skeptical. If no one talks about possible career paths at the organization, they may assume that the only option is what's directly above them.

That's how it was for me at Cornerstone. There was never a career path conversation with me. I'm a go-getter guy and I wanted to get promoted. I wanted to understand what was next for me. So because there was never a discussion around a career path, my assumption was that there were no opportunities other than Senior Accountant of Revenue at Cornerstone. Maybe that's just me being paranoid, automatically assuming the worst case scenario, but that was a big reason I left.

That means you need to find ways to continually encourage your team to punch above their weight. You've got to sit down with them and create a concrete path forward to help them reach their own career goals while helping the company reach its goals.

The days of getting a college degree and having a set job for life with a clear ascension up the corporate ladder are long over, if that was ever really a thing. Millennials embrace flexibility, so the best way forward for each person may not be what's above them in the company org chart.

LET YOUR PEOPLE MOVE AROUND

Besides hiring great people, another key to employee retention is having managers who really understand their team's strengths and weaknesses, and giving team members new opportunities in areas where they might be strong. A prime example is Troy Patipanavat, an accountant who started out as a Customer Success Representative, and is now moving to a completely different part of our company:

> *I started my first job in public accounting as an auditor for BDO, and I did that for two years. After two years, I knew I wanted to pivot into a new career where I could work in a client-facing role and provide value. People run away from auditors, and it was hard to see the value-add in that type of profession, especially at such a young age.*
>
> *One day I came across FloQast on a Google search of keywords "Lakers + Accounting" and then I came across FloQast's Twitter account. After researching about FloQast, I realized how powerful a tool FloQast was.*
>
> *At FloQast, I started out working in Customer Success. We had an*

experimental team where I would set up new clients for outsourced accounting firms on our software. I worked closely with CPO Chris Sluty, who gave me a lot of autonomy in managing my own clients. In public accounting, autonomy was rarely given. I worked for several seniors and managers who micro-managed, which takes away the freedom of expression when making decisions, thus impeding personal development.

I've been empowered to dabble in sales by going to on-site product demos. I've also been part of sales negotiation calls with our CEO Mike, our Director of Sales, Adam Zoucha, Account Executive Alex Gillingham, and the prospects' CFO, CEO, and Director of Accounting. This really challenged me to understand the full sales cycle from start to end, as well as skillsets involving presentation and negotiation skills.

Then the most distinct opportunity came when Chris pulled me to the side and asked if I would be interested in helping with FloQast's social media account. While the team saw the value I added as a Customer Success Representative, Chris and Mike saw the greater value-add potential I could contribute as a full-time member of the Social Media team. That's when Mike came over and presented me with this opportunity to leap into a completely new field full time. What started out as an invitation to help assist the social media team, eventually turned into a full-time opportunity.

I was completely grateful because it's not everyday that you work for open minded executives who allow their own employees to pivot to their strengths. When Mike and Chris see a value-added opportunity that would generate greater growth for the company, they would initiate on it.

Mike and Chris are great at finding what people are best at and putting them in positions that match their strengths to succeed. This is why I've been here for 2.8 years now, which is a long time, in the start-up world at least. I've been challenged in a multitude of different ways that allowed me to grow professionally.

> *Providing employees with new challenges, and putting team members where they best fit, allows FloQast to be very innovative, agile, and most importantly, to build a dynamic work environment that retains top employees.*

You don't have to do something as radical as the move that Troy is making. It can be as simple as giving someone a different balance sheet account to work on. If you have someone working on deferred revenue, that person is going to get bored booking only those journal entries. As nerdy as it sounds, move that person to capitalized software. It's a new challenge. Take some liberties and allow your team to work across the balance sheet. And then, by the way, you're going to have a better team that understands accounting more broadly.

TAKE A WRECKING BALL TO YOUR ORG CHART

The future leaders of your organization could care less about their exact job title and the upward rungs to climb the corporate ladder. They may make multiple lateral or diagonal moves to gain experience in different parts of the company, and they have little patience for people promoted up the ladder beyond their zone of competency.

Rigid job descriptions with no alternative means of moving up won't work anymore. Just saying "that's the way I came up through the ranks, so that's the way everyone needs to do it too" won't cut it. Instead, future-oriented organizations are creating org charts based on the tasks or functions needed, not the job title. And software will be a position in that org chart.

At one extreme are large organizations where simple decisions to buy a piece of software take months of navigating countless layers of bureaucracy. That sounds like some of the big CPA firms that some of our team members worked at. At the other end of the spectrum are companies like Zappos with a flat, self-managed structure called a "holacracy." Both types of organizations create distinct challenges for employees and leaders alike. Maybe your organization is somewhere in the middle.

As a recent article in the Wall Street Journal[32] reports, "when AI does the routine tasks, much of the remaining nonroutine work is likely to be done in loose 'adhocracies,' ever-shifting groups of people with the combinations of skills needed for whatever problems arise." It's possible that in many organizations in the future, informal teams will come together to work on a project, and when the project is complete, the team will disband, and members will join other teams to work on different projects.

As FloQast has grown, we've created different levels of management. But everyone is still accountable to their team members, and our commitment to transparency enables that. We also encourage cross-departmental collaboration, and have several programs that help people learn what the different departments do.

A NEW SHAPE FOR YOUR ORG CHART

The traditional pyramid shaped org chart — where a veritable army at the bottom level reports to a smaller management layer above them, and so on, until you reach the top — is disappearing, in case you hadn't noticed. According to the AICPA and CGMA,[33] the future shape for organizations will be more like a hexagon, or almost diamond shaped, with the biggest group of employees somewhere in the middle, not at the bottom.

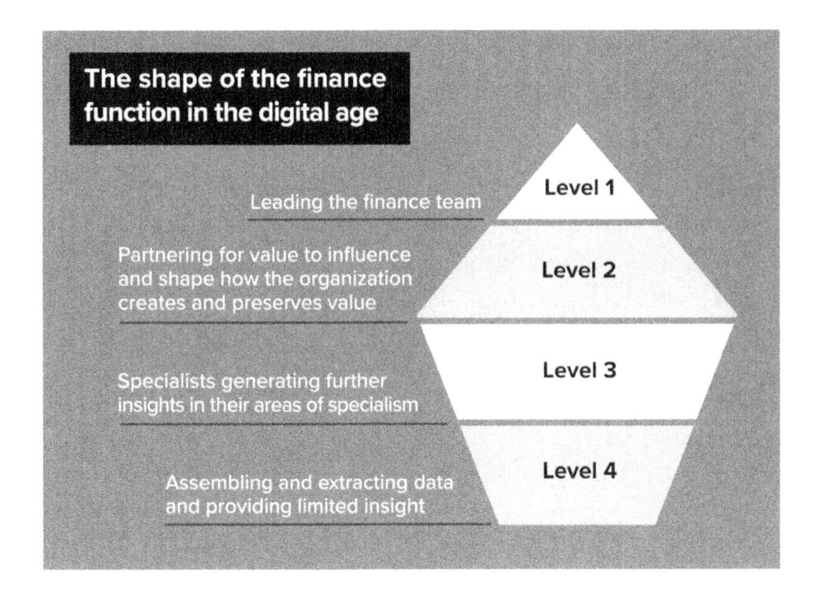

Automation and outsourcing are already reducing the number of people needed at the very bottom level of organizations, and this trend won't stop. A recent report by the Brookings Institution[34] on the future impacts of automation and AI notes that the impact will be most keenly felt in occupations with a high proportion of "routine, predictable physical and cognitive tasks," with office administration jobs being among the most vulnerable.

Looking back at the impact of automation over the last 30 years, the researchers found that "automation in the last 30 years delivered more jobs to the economy than it destroyed, and so holds out significant opportunity." And while automation substitutes for tasks done by humans rather than replacing entire occupations, the authors feel that there is a limit — machines will never do it all. There will still be "a persistent need for human labor, even in highly automated contexts." So we will see more humans working alongside technology.

I saw this first-hand at EY, where we had technology backed

up with low-cost offshore teams who were doing the bank recs and cash audits for us. We had teams that were mostly seniors, and one staff overseeing the offshore team, which gave us a more diamond-shaped organization.

As the function of accounting and finance departments shifts from assembling and reporting information to being a business partner for the whole organization, this broader focus requires more people in the middle who interact with the business as a whole, and fewer people at the bottom processing data.

TREAT YOUR PEOPLE WELL AND THEY'LL TREAT YOU WELL

Solving the challenges with people starts with getting the right people on the bus and getting them in the right seats on that bus, to paraphrase Jim Collins. Keeping them on your bus means having a flexible approach, with your eye on the big Why for your organization, and always advocating for your team members, guiding and mentoring them to become the best they can be. That flexible approach also means being willing to move people to completely different parts of your organization, and supporting them in the learning they need to excel.

But as I find in leading a growing team at FloQast, having the best people with the best skills and giving them the training and resources they need to keep improving won't get you the results you need unless you also add in the next ingredient in our Culture equation: Trust.

6 / TRUST IS THE GLUE THAT BUILDS TEAMS

The best way to find out if you can trust somebody is to trust them.
–Ernest Hemingway

Big Four accountants are competitive, but I was fortunate to be on good teams during my time at EY. We had a powerful team mentality. We supported each other. We helped each other. We trusted each other. My senior manager had a rule that we would all leave at the same time every night. If you finished your work early, then you would take on more work rather than sit around and twiddle your thumbs. That way, everyone could leave earlier.

But at Cornerstone, there was not much of a team mentality when I started. People were given their own work, and they worked in their own bubbles. There was nothing like FloQast, where you could understand what other people were working on. So you went home whenever you were done with your work. Because they gave me the harder stuff to work on, I would be working significantly later than many other people at the organization. I would be there until 11 every night during the close.

I've heard similar horror stories from my other CPA friends. Places where backstabbing, malicious gossip, and taking credit for someone else's idea were the norm. Where management made sweeping changes that blindsided everyone. Those are all signs of a workplace culture that lacks trust.

One definition of trust is the reciprocal extension of vulnerability to another. In the workplace, this is demonstrated by team members who know that if they ask for help, someone will help them, and that asking for help won't be seen as a sign of weakness, or be held against you.

The Gallup Organization's work with engagement in the workplace identifies trust and support as essential elements for creating highly engaged employees, and notes that "Employees need to be in an environment where there are mutual trust and respect for one another's efforts and results."[1]

Paul Zak, a neuroscience researcher who studies the relationship between events in the brain and the impact on the workplace, found that trust can have a huge impact on the bottom line: "Compared with people at low-trust companies, people at high-trust companies report: 74% less stress, 106% more energy at work, 50% higher productivity, 13% fewer sick days,

76% more engagement, 29% more satisfaction with their lives, 40% less burnout."[2] All of that sounds like a place where I want to work.

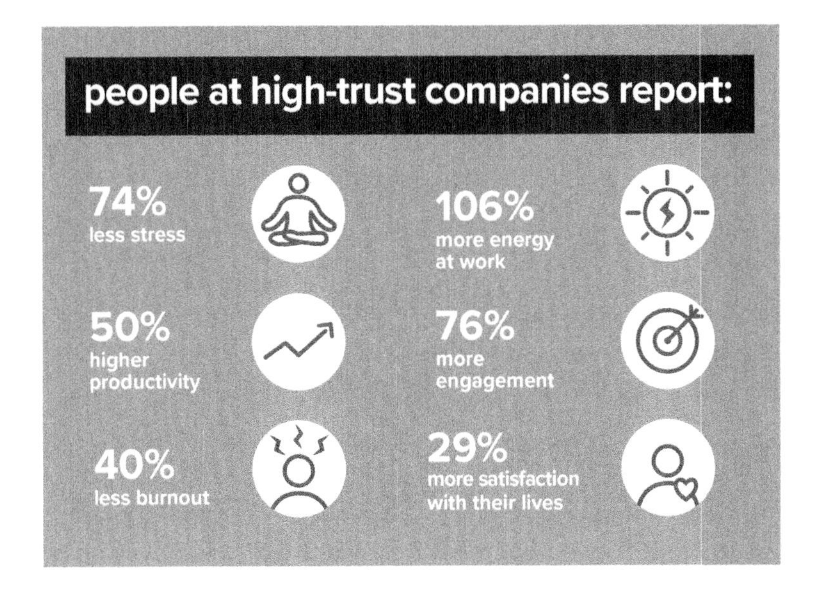

But a lot of workplaces aren't like that. In 2014, the American Psychological Association surveyed 1,564 people across the US, and found that about one-quarter don't trust their employer.[3] About one in three don't think their employer is always honest and truthful. Ouch. I am sure some of you reading this book have worked at places like that, especially if you spent time in public accounting.

Trust is an ingredient in creating a highly engaged team. In 2018, the ADP Research Institute looked at engagement in 19 countries to identify what conditions are most likely to attract and retain talented employees. Those research findings are detailed and expanded on in the book *Nine Lies About Work*. The ADP researchers found that "by far the best explainer of engagement levels was whether or not the team members trusted their leader."[4] Those who trusted their team leaders were twelve times more likely to have the highest levels of engagement than those who did not.

So how do we create a high-trust workplace? This will first and foremost require leadership skills. Managing people isn't a core skill taught to accountants, but today's younger workforce have zero tolerance for a poor culture, and they'll be quick to exit if they can't trust their co-workers or managers. And with their talents in high demand, you risk losing those hard-to-replace team members if you don't create a high-trust environment.

So let's take a look at leadership skills as a way to build trust in the workplace.

MANAGERS ARE BECOMING LEADERS

Leadership isn't something that's usually taught alongside GAAP and consolidations. But as a controller, you need to be competent both at technical accounting and managing a team. Leadership is how you create culture. It's how everyone stays focused on the Why for the organization.

Have you ever worked under someone who was promoted to be a manager because they were good at the technical aspects of their job, but who had no clue about leading a team? One of those stereotypical introverted accountants who prefers spreadsheets to people? Most of us have.

The modern controller is different. He or she must be the glue that holds your department and company culture together. A big part of that glue is trust.

HOW I'VE LEARNED TO BE A LEADER

Contrary to what the promoters of MBA programs tell us, you won't learn leadership by getting an MBA. You might learn a lot of theory, but to become a great leader, you've actually got to try this stuff out in the real world. I'm a big believer in learning by doing, so here are the ways I've learned leadership.

SPORTS AND THE ART OF WAR

I played a lot of sports growing up, and I wasn't the most skilled guy. But I worked the hardest and tried the hardest, so I was chosen as team captain more times than I can remember. That's how I learned the power of leading by example. I also learned how to create a team environment.

A big thing that came out of sports is how to leverage competition or focus on a common enemy to drive greater teamwork. A competitive spirit really rallies everyone to pull together to do what it takes, whatever it takes, to take out that enemy.

The common enemy tactic still works for me. Since I founded FloQast, I've always disliked our biggest competitor. So I rally the salespeople and everyone in the company so that we can be the David that beats the Goliath. Internally, the departments might not get along, and not everyone in every department may get along, but at the end of the day, the real fight is with that outside business. So we pull together as a company to be better than the competition and beat them.

This sports strategy is used everywhere. I read *The Art of War* recently, which was written around the 5th century BC by master military strategist Sun Tzu. One of the tactics in *The Art of War* is to leverage a common enemy. It's kind of funny, though, that I've met a couple of VPs of Sales who have talked about this idea of leveraging a common enemy as some kind of top-secret business tactic that was just recently discovered. To me, it just seems like common sense. I don't know why more people don't use this tactic.

IMPROVE YOUR SPEAKING SKILLS BY JOINING TOASTMASTERS

When I first founded FloQast, I was pretty terrible at public speaking. Like most people, and like most accountants in particular, I didn't have much practice at it. It's not something they teach along with revenue recognition.

But I knew that public speaking was something I needed to improve at. So I joined Toastmasters and went to meetings for a couple months. At Toastmasters, I found a super supportive environment. Everyone there was just trying to get better at public speaking. We would have practice sessions, and critique each other. It was a very trusting environment. What I loved most was that I learned the specific areas I needed to work on.

It was really helpful. It gave me confidence that I'm actually not as bad at public speaking as I thought I was.

Because controllers straddle two worlds: the technical accounting world and the bigger world of business, they need to be able to communicate well with both sides, as Brandt Kucharski, CAO of Grubhub says:

> *The table stakes, just to be a chief accountant, you have to be as technical as anyone else. You have to be able to speak that language to your auditors and to external parties that deal in that route.*
>
> *However, when you speak to other people in technology and marketing and human resources, you have to be able to convey a message that leads to common understanding. You can't be just quoting 606 or other accounting standards. You have to have the ability to really demonstrate why something is important. If you just go to the actual guidance and read out the passage, that message will just get lost.*

This means accountants need to be able to translate the language of numbers and the convoluted FASB guidance into simple language that non-accountants can understand.

TEACH YOUR TEAM HOW TO SUCCEED ON THEIR OWN

Whether we know it or not, one way we accountants get trained in leadership is by example. As an auditor, you're being given work that's one level ahead of your actual title. When you're a staff accountant, the senior on the job will give you senior level work. The response of the senior is usually to get in the trenches with you and show you how to do the work. Then, when you get to be a senior, you provide the same hands-on training for the staff person under you.

But by the time you get to the manager level, you've got to really change how you work with your team. Not changing is a common first year management mistake. You're used to working like a senior, being in the trenches, really doing in depth reviewing, and because you're really good at it, you just keep doing that. Unfortunately, that's why most new managers are so overworked.

But that's not really what a good manager is. A good manager is not someone who can help you do the work. It's someone who can help you get good at doing the work on your own, and then help you build your career from there. It's someone who trusts that you'll be able to develop those skills. Someone who's willing to help you set goals and achieve them, and who doesn't need to micromanage to make sure that you do it in exactly the same way that they would.

This is a big challenge. And specifically one I've been dealing with as we've been adding new layers of management at FloQast. The new managers have a different mentality from the experienced managers.

New managers tend to be protective of their poor performers. The best thing you can do with a poor performer is focus on them and try to make them better in the short term. If that doesn't work, it's best to just cut them loose and move on.

But instead, new managers will often try to cover up that person's performance. They'll do some of that person's work for them instead of bringing it to my attention and accepting that this person isn't a good employee so we can move on.

I understand why these new managers act this way. They think that this poor performer is a poor reflection on their management skills, and as an audit senior, that's what we were taught.

The reality is that you can't make every poor performer into a productive employee. A 50% success rate is great. That means half the time, it's a bad hire, and it's much better to acknowledge that and move on rather than keeping that person and trying to make it work.

ASK MORE QUESTIONS THAN YOU ANSWER (SOMETIMES)

This is a tough one for accountants, especially when we come from the public accounting world, where we're taught to always have the answers ready. As accountants, we don't like to look vulnerable by showing our lack of knowledge. If we're in a low-trust environment, we're scared that if we don't know everything, that might derail our careers.

Asking good questions takes a lot of thought, which takes a lot of time. And time isn't something we accountants have much of. But when you ask the right questions, it helps your team figure out the right answer themselves and learn how to solve the problem in the future. You have to trust that they will figure out the right answer.

But Chris and I concede that this doesn't work for everyone. Some people like a lot of autonomy and are really self-driven, so they'll figure things out on their own, with maybe a little guidance. Asking them the right questions inspires them to find creative and innovative solutions. As long as they don't try to reinvent the wheel, so to speak.

There are others who don't like so much autonomy. Some people prefer to make decisions within a framework. When I work with these kinds of people — and this has to do with adapting to different personalities — I've found it works best to point them firmly in the right direction and give them a couple of options. Either of those options are the right answer, but it's up to them to choose the one they want to pursue.

BE A CHEETAH, NOT A LAMB

Back in the 2000s, the authors of *Who: The A Method for Hiring* teamed up with some researchers to analyze whether there was a perfect profile of a successful CEO. They came up with two main profiles: the Lambs and the Cheetahs.

Lambs are more of the "servant-leader" type. They ask questions, they're respectful, and boards and investors really like to work with them. As the authors say, "we call them 'Lambs' because these CEOs tend to graze in circles, feeding on the feedback and direction of others."

Cheetahs, on the other hand, "move quickly, act aggressively, work hard, demonstrate persistence, and set high standards and hold people accountable to them. We call these CEOs 'Cheetahs' because they are fast and focused."

The researchers found there was a significant difference in the financial performance of companies led by these two kinds of CEOs. The Lambs, on average, produced positive results for investors 57% of the time. That's not shabby.

But the Cheetahs were successful 100% of the time. Every single Cheetah in the study produced value for the investors.

When I read that book, it was really a turning point for me. I had been trying to be more of a Lamb, even though that's not my natural style. But I didn't like how things were going.

So now I'm trying to find balance. When we have a meeting now, I'll throw something out there. I'll let everyone else in the room argue. I'll chime in as I deem necessary and I'll ask questions, to spur the conversation. Then if everyone agrees, and we get to an answer, that's great. We got there naturally, and I didn't have to tell anyone what to do.

If there's any debate at the end, then I'll make the decision after hearing everyone out. We have smart executives, and I want to hear their feedback. But let's just get to the right answer.

The problem I see with the Lamb style of leadership is that it can create an organization where you have a lack of decisiveness. And when you have a lack of decisiveness, you don't get as much done.

So my balance between the Lamb and the Cheetah is to allow for disagreement, then make a decision and commit to going in this direction.

Review Note: Seek out mentors and be a mentor yourself

Fewer relationships are more valuable to learning leadership than the one you have with a mentor. The best mentors model the behaviors you want to improve on and help you. They can make a difference in your life, and your approach to leading. That's what Brandt Kucharski, CAO of Grubhub found in his mentor, Bob Berti, when he was at Crowe.

> *I was fortunate enough to have a really good mentor when I was back in public accounting before Grubhub. From day one, Bob Berti took me under his wing. He showed me that if you really want to excel in business, you have to be a leader, and you have to inspire people and motivate them to do things.*
>
> *Stop yelling at them. That won't get the best work out of them.*

You really have to be that visionary that people look up to and that people want to be around. Then you're able to really motivate people and get them to really bring the best work product that they can do.

At your organization or perhaps in your community, there may be people who exemplify what you want to become. The best mentorship relationships are two-way, where both sides get something out of it. So before you approach someone and ask them to be a mentor to you, consider what you could possibly bring to the relationship. Maybe it's the finer points of understanding how accounting standards impact the financials, or maybe you're connected to people who would help them.

Actively seeking out mentorship is one of the primary ways that Derek Mernagh, controller at Yelp, has been able to become an effective leader. Besides reaching out to his CFO for guidance in challenges he faces, he looks to a network of peers that he stays in contact with through regular meetings for coffee, drinks, or dinner.

> *By reaching out to my network of previous bosses and people in similar positions at other companies and asking them how they tackled certain things has really helped to gain insight into how other people have navigated similar challenges. That mentorship thing is really important.*

Mentors can also be found in great business books. Dale Carnegie's classic *How to Win Friends and Influence People* is an obvious one. Another one is *The Seven Habits of Highly Successful People* by Stephen Covey.

FIND YOUR WHY

It's almost a cliche to quote Simon Sinek and the importance of finding the core reason for doing your business, but finding my Why is the reason I founded FloQast: to find a better way for controllers and finance teams to close the books.

When you find your Why, and project that out to the company, and to the public, you'll attract the kinds of people to work for you who will move heaven and earth to make that Why a reality. You don't want to hire people who just want a job. You want to hire people who want to make a difference.

I remember when I was at Cornerstone, our CEO was really good explaining that the reason we were working so hard was because we wanted to become the biggest talent management company in the space. We would have these town hall meetings and he would give us the visionary thing. I remember leaving and being all excited about what we were doing as a business. It made me a little more excited to do my job, even though as the revenue guy, I wasn't really contributing on a huge level. But it felt fun to be part of a company that was doing well in Los Angeles.

Remember what I said earlier about Millennial customers who value empathy over arrogance? The new generation of accountants care more about why your company exists, and why the accounting department needs to serve that greater good than they do about paychecks (although paychecks are also awfully important!).

So find your Why, talk about it, write about it, and make it the focus for the accounting department, and you'll build a loyal tribe of high performers.

SPEND MORE TIME WITH YOUR HIGH PERFORMERS THAN YOUR LOW PERFORMERS

This may seem the opposite of the way we're usually taught to mentor our team, but it will pay off big time. With a little extra encouragement and mentoring, your high performers can become the superstars of your team. Maybe they'll ultimately take on a different leadership role in the company and work beside you as an equal. Or maybe they'll move to another company, which can often be a positive. That connection to another organization may lead to other opportunities for you, or for other members of your team, or that person may send you the team member you need, who's just not a good fit for their team.

Plus, look at what you're rewarding with your time and attention — exactly the behaviors you want to see.

It's true that with some extra attention and targeted coaching, some of your low performers will step up to the plate and hit a home run. Maybe they'll transform into high performers. Most of them won't.

When you spend more time with the bottom of your team, it sends a signal to the rest of your team that the way to get attention from you is to be a slacker.

LEARN HOW TO ARGUE, NOT FIGHT

When my co-founder Cullen and I both read *Thank You for Arguing* by Jay Heinrichs, our working relationship completely changed. That book takes a lot of the conversational and argumentative tactics I've naturally used over the years, and modifies them to magnify their persuasive power.

It taught me how to get my point across, and how to persuade other people to do what I wanted them to do, without being a bully. I learned how to argue, not fight. As Heinrichs says, "The basic difference between an argument and a fight: an argument, done skillfully, gets people to do what you want. You fight to win; you argue to achieve agreement."

This is a book on rhetoric that has really helped me step back from any discussion that was heading into confrontational waters, and guide it where I needed it to go. I use these ideas when I talk to investors, to the board, to the executive team, and to the whole team. I even use these ideas on my wife, but don't tell her!

LEADERSHIP IS A BALANCING ACT

As a controller, you're smack in the middle of two opposing groups. Below you are your team of accountants, who are deep in the weeds of accounting transactions. Above you is the C-suite, who need a bigger picture view. Here's how John Gammon, Global Controller at Ancestry manages that balancing act:

> *Delegation is always important to make sure you get out of the weeds. When you're a controller, there's a certain level of "weeding," that's necessary within your role. When you get into the details of reviewing journal entries or reconciliations, you have to be able to understand what's in the depths of those things.*
>
> *But you have to be able to delegate as much as you can to your managers and other team members. They should be able to handle most of that stuff. So you can take more of a high level approach.*
>
> *You also have to make sure you take a high level approach when you're talking with the owners of the business itself, because they're not going to want to talk about the weeds. You have to deal with it from a compliance perspective, You have to be able to speak intelligently to the business owners throughout the business. And at a high level so you can make sure that you understand where they're coming from, and then be able to translate that into what the accountants on your team are doing.*
>
> *You're kind of the liaison between the line level accountants and the business owners.*

BUILD TRUST BY TRUSTING OTHERS

Having a great team is only a part of the culture equation. To build a powerful workplace culture, those people need to have trust on many levels.

They need to trust that their co-workers won't stab them in

the back, and won't betray confidences or spread malicious gossip. They need to feel supported by their team, and that they are all working toward the same Why.

They need to trust that their managers and other team members have their best interests at heart, and aren't just using them. They need to feel that their ideas matter.

The best way to get people to trust you is to extend trust to others. That takes a certain level of maturity, especially when you hire a specialist with strong domain expertise in their functional area. Trusting that the people under you know their particular area better than you do was a key for Jerry Raphael, CFO of StackOverflow, when he suddenly had to step up his game.

> *When our CFO left the business in 2017, I stepped up immediately and took on a lot of the responsibilities without even being asked. The most difficult part was not being accustomed to all the different functional areas I suddenly became responsible for. I was the controller, and overnight, I was responsible for HR, legal, sales operations, and office facilities functions, effectively supporting the broader business functions for a late stage growth company. So, it was a rather tough learning curve.*
>
> *I spent a lot of time with each of the functional teams, listening and learning about what they did and their approach to their roles. In the end, I had to trust the directors of those groups to lead the way. They were employed as subject matter experts and I needed to give them space to perform their roles and support them by removing as many obstacles and barriers for them to succeed.*

As you move up in an organization, there's just no way you can have your finger on every piece of the work below you. You have to trust them to do the work, and do it well. As I've found, hiring people who can teach you something is a powerful key to building a strong organization. You don't want to be the smartest person in the room.

DELEGATING WORK IS THE BEST WAY FOR YOUR TEAM TO LEARN

I believe that the best way to learn is by doing, so delegating work is the best way for your team to learn. Delegation can be scary, especially when you've done something the same way for a long time. But remember, the main reason to hire new people is so they can take work off your (or someone else on your team's) plate so that you have time and energy to do higher level work. If you've hired people who are better than you at the job, delegation is a no-brainer. You can trust them to do the work. Sure, they might have a different approach, but if they find an easier, faster, and more accurate way to do it, everybody wins.

One way to delegate is to assign projects to people on your team. There's just no way for a controller to keep up with all the special projects you could do. But if someone expresses an interest in a project, then let them take ownership of it.

The keys to delegation are trust and accountability. If you don't trust that someone's going to do the work well, and if you don't have any means of accountability, then you'll be stuck micromanaging them to make sure the work gets done. On the other hand, if you hire people who are proactive, who are self-starters, then obviously, the results will be much better.

One of my goals when Cullen, Chris, and I founded FloQast was to help controllers get the bandwidth to spend more time on the important work and less time on the boring, manual work. Here's what Shivang Patel, Director of Sales Engineering, says about how controllers can achieve that, and keep their best people at the same time.

During the close, a controller should spend 90% of their time reviewing, and 10% on data entry. Or maybe it's 80:20, but less time than they are now. How do we achieve that? We achieve that through systems, automation, good talented people, and then just knowing what you need to do for your process to be efficient. It's not going to happen overnight. If the long term goal is to be more qualitatively accurate, then you need to push more responsibilities to your staff members. Accountants will leave if they don't get valuable, rewarding work. They'll go somewhere else.

Good people want to do interesting work. The way you keep your good people is by giving them things to do that take them out of the day to day. But as a controller, how can you do that if you're spending 90% of your time in data entry?

Delegation done well demonstrates to your team that you trust them to do the work just as well as you do, or maybe better. Delegation can get your people excited about their jobs because they're challenged to step up their game. Doing work that's just a little beyond your abilities makes you stretch. I remember when I started getting one-off projects at Cornerstone, I got really excited about the stuff I got to do. I was assigned the Sarbanes Oxley implementation, and they didn't have to sit me down and explain every step. They just asked me if I could help them get SOX compliant. That was a really fun project because I had free rein to make it happen.

But there are things you have to be careful about delegating, as John Gammon, Global Controller of Ancestry says. I asked him what would be the last things he would delegate off his plate, and here's what he told me:

Final approvals for your AP check run, or your payroll would be the last things I would delegate. And final approvals for things like contract reviews where it requires a certain level of understanding of the really big picture to see what's going on. It's not that someone on your team couldn't do it, but before you delegate that to them, you've got to make sure that you are crystal clear on what your expectations are and what review procedures need to happen before those approvals are given.

Anything where there's cash going out the door, or that requires a business understanding, you probably want to be part of the approval process.

TRY A BOTTOMS-UP APPROACH INSTEAD OF TOP-DOWN

We accountants tend to be resistant to change. As FloQast Product Manager Erika Hecksher says, a large degree of that resistance comes from our training. But trusting that the people on your team will come up with ideas on how to make things better opens the door to real change.

The people who end up in accounting are a self-selected group. Many of them come out of audit, and are trained pretty hard to do it the same way it was done last year, or SALY. While SALY is considered to be a way to reduce risk, I think it's really a bad approach.

I recognize the impact it has in an audit environment. If I change my spreadsheet, my reviewer has to change the way he does things. My whole budget for the audit is in danger of being blown. I get that.

But when you're in a corporate environment, you don't have that same situation. There are people who go into accounting who are interested in technology. Most of them have a very fancy smartphone that they play with a lot. They're very tech savvy. Some of them are really interested in really changing the systems around them.

Encouraging these tech savvy people to serve a bottoms-up approach as opposed to a top-down control approach can really change an accounting department. The top-down control approach is very tempting, but I don't think it truly gives you control. It just gives you SALY.

> *It doesn't give you any innovation and any improvement in your process. It won't help you as a controller achieve any of your objectives, because your objectives by nature embody change.*
>
> *If you want change, you have to create an environment for your staff that allows them to change and encourages them to find better ways of doing things.*

TRUST YOUR TEAM AND THEY'LL TRUST YOU

A great team of people you can trust, and who trust each other and the leaders of the business (including yourself), will get you part of the way towards creating a great culture. But to build a truly great culture, you need the final element of our equation: accountability. That's what we'll be looking at now.

Accountability should be seen as a positive impact on an organization, not the blame game for when something goes wrong.

7 / ACCOUNTABILITY ISN'T JUST COMPLIANCE

Not everything that can be counted counts, and not everything that counts can be counted.
—William Bruce Cameron

Through our training, accountants learn to be disciplined, detail-oriented, and cautious. Negligence can be deadly to our careers, if not to our organizations. Some things just cannot be wrong. In our work, we sign off on workpapers. Our work goes through multiple levels of review. We have to make sure that the mistakes get fixed before the work goes out the door.

As accountants, it may be natural that we consider accountability to be a matter of compliance. And in the world outside of our jobs, when there's a terrible industrial accident, or some gross misconduct that harms many others, such as the wrong-headed financial incentives that led to the collapse of the housing market and the Great Recession, we want to find someone to attach blame to — someone who can be held accountable for the problem.

But thinking about accountability just in terms of compliance misses the potential for positive impact that this can have on our organizations. Back in 2014, Partners in Leadership published results of an exhaustive survey of over 40,000 people they did on accountability (Sadly, only the executive summary seems to be available now). They found that most people have accountability wrong. According to their survey, "The data overwhelmingly shows that the practice of accountability in the workplace has resulted in the view that accountability is something that happens to you when things go wrong, rather than something you do to yourself to ensure results."[1]

An astounding 80% of respondents reported that feedback only happened when something went wrong, so accountability was after-the-fact or punitive. Part of this may have to do with the lack of awareness that those surveyed had of their organizations' Why: fully 85% said they weren't sure what their organizations were trying to achieve.

Accountability isn't just about making sure that those reporting to you have done all the work assigned to them. Like trust, accountability works best when it's reciprocal, and when you create a workplace culture where people want to do their best work. As corporate change consultant Randy Pennington wrote on the SHRM website:

> Leaders who struggle with others' accountability view their job as mandating compliance. Those who get accountability right know that most people want to do great work. They view their job as creating an environment where commitment and self-discipline are volunteered.[2]

TRUST AND ACCOUNTABILITY CREATE A COLLABORATIVE CULTURE

By building a culture of trust, you are creating transparency. Transparency enables accountability. When everyone has visibility into what everyone else is doing, you can create a culture where people want to do great work, and where collaboration is second nature.

In team sports, everyone can see what everyone else's strengths and weaknesses are because the team practices together. And because that team has the same goal — winning — then everyone is accountable to everyone else to be the best they can be.

Remember from our discussion of trust, this is a reciprocal relationship. If your people don't (or can't) trust you, their level of commitment to the organization plummets.

ACCOUNTABILITY STARTS FROM THE TOP

This culture of collaboration, transparency, and accountability absolutely has to come from the top. As General George Patton said, "Do everything you ask of those you command." When your team sees you working with others, sharing your goals, and being accountable in reaching them, that gives them a model for the behaviors and attitudes that will get them ahead in your organization.

Employees know this implicitly. According to the Partners in Leadership study on accountability, "84% of those surveyed cite the way leaders behave as the single most important factor accountability influence in their organizations."

Accountability means being open and honest yourself. You have to have the self-confidence that when you make a mistake, admitting it won't be fatal. Admitting a mistake, proposing a solution, and moving on will raise your stature in the eyes of your team.

Another crucial part of this is actually following through on your promises. If you tell someone they need to do X to be promoted or get a raise, and they do it, you've got to follow through. Otherwise, you'll lose the trust of your whole team.

VISIBILITY LEADS TO ACCOUNTABILITY

Setting clear expectations is key to creating an accountable culture. That's why we created a dashboard in FloQast, so everyone has visibility into the workflow. When everyone can see where the bottlenecks are, who's getting the work done, and who's not, this encourages your hard workers to step up their game. It also fosters teamwork and helping team members cooperate to get the work done. This is similar to the teamwork I experienced at EY, when my manager had the rule that everyone went home at the same time.

DELETE THE BLAME CULTURE

Many leaders wrongly view accountability as something that cascades down from the top and only hits the people at the bottom. This was definitely the case with Wells Fargo, when senior leadership initially escaped culpability for the incentives that led to as many as 3.5 million fake accounts being created.[3]

While incentives for performance can inspire people to work hard, they also need to be realistic. Wells Fargo imposed impossible sales quotas on their front-line employees, who resorted to creating fake accounts to reach them. When the scandal broke, CEO John Stumpf blamed the front-line employees for misunderstanding their sales goals.

That's not the kind of culture you want. It takes real leadership to step up and take responsibility when there's a systemic failure like that. It's so much easier to point fingers and look for someone else — anyone else — to blame when things go wrong. As Brandt Kucharski, CAO of Grubhub learned from his mentor, effective leadership means you "stop yelling at them."

I believe failures like the one at Wells Fargo happen when leadership forgets that accountability goes two ways. While it's true that employees need to fulfill their responsibilities to leaders, leaders also need to be accountable to their employees to make sure that fulfilling those responsibilities isn't going to harm them, or result in behaviors you don't want.

Now I'm not saying that you should ignore wilful acts or when someone does something worthy of termination. That's when you show them the door. But I do believe that when something goes massively wrong, that's when you need to look at the context of events that allowed that to happen. Maybe there are policies or procedures that need to be examined. Maybe there's a genuine misunderstanding of what leaders wanted to have happen. But without looking at the context of why something happened, you don't have the opportunity to learn from it and make sure it doesn't happen again.

ACCOUNTABILITY IS NOT PUNISHMENT

Accountability shouldn't be wielded like a sword over someone's head when they make a mistake. The object in being a great leader is to help your people become better human beings. So instead of yelling at someone and asking them "How could you do this?" it's more productive to ask "How did this happen?" and "What can we do to keep this from happening again?" You have to be willing to forgive mistakes, learn from them, and move on.

Accountability is best when it's used as a way to measure progress towards a goal, and when it's used as a measure to encourage the kinds of behaviors you want to see. You do want to have consequences when someone doesn't do what they said they would do, otherwise, those goals become meaningless and everyone ignores them. Ultimately, if someone can't hit their goals, maybe the goals need revision, or maybe they need help.

Your team will feel better about admitting mistakes and being accountable for the consequences when they see that behavior modeled from the top. This to me is the highest level of accountability: when you point to yourself and take responsibility for a problem instead of pointing down the line to someone else.

ACCOUNTABILITY MAKES TEAMS STRONGER

In team sports, the team members are accountable to each other to perform, and to work together, or the team as a whole doesn't win. It's a reciprocal relationship. Everyone depends on each other to do what everyone has committed to.

In the workplace, team members are not only accountable to fulfill their commitments, but they also need to hold each other accountable. The best teams aren't merely asking for the bare minimum contribution: they're expecting the best performance from each other. They are clear on what each person needs to contribute and they encourage each other.

Weak teams have no accountability. It's a free for all. Chaos, nothing gets done, and there's plenty of back stabbing.

One step up, and mediocre teams have accountability imposed by the boss, and by the boss alone. Accountability is punitive. Everyone is ready to throw someone under the bus to stay out of trouble.

Strong teams are accountable to each other. Team members don't hesitate to call each other out when something gets missed. But they also have each other's backs. It's sort of a tough love situation, but everyone knows they are doing their part to create something bigger than themselves.

Calling each other out right away instead of wondering why someone didn't do their job makes the relationship stronger. Holding it back can lead to distrust and a toxic workplace.

The challenge, though, is to make sure that when you're calling someone out, you're doing it in a constructive way, and in a way that reflects how best to manage them.

GET HONEST FEEDBACK (EVEN WHEN IT HURTS)

Giving and getting feedback are important in leadership. But getting honest feedback from your reports can be tricky. They might feel that their job could be in jeopardy if they really tell the truth. But as John Gammon, Global Controller at Ancestry, discovered, there's one time that's perfect for getting really honest feedback.

> *I think it's important to solicit 360 degree feedback, especially from departing employees. One of the best conversations that I ever had was when I was leaving a company. I spoke with one of my direct reports, someone I had worked with for probably five years. And I said, "Hey, there are no repercussions here. Give it to me straight, Tell me what you like and don't like about working with me."*
>
> *And she had some very candid, pointed feedback for me, and it was hard to take. But it was really important to just accept it at face value and say, "Okay, well, what can I learn from this?" A lot of it was pretty hard to receive. But it was very true.*
>
> *And so as a manager, if you are leaving to go somewhere else, or if you have an employee who's leaving your company to go somewhere else, you may as well encourage that person, or a direct report, if you're the one leaving, to give you the feedback that they can.*
>
> *So many times, direct reports are scared to give their managers feedback along the way, especially if it's negative feedback, because they think it's going to impact their performance reviews and the types of opportunities they may have going forward. They may view it as a career limiting move.*
>
> *But the feedback I got was so valuable that I would definitely want to*

hire that person again. I know that she'll tell it to me straight. There were times that she'd give me feedback along the way. But it was even more pointed at the very end.

Encouraging that kind of honesty from your team is hard. You want to be able to solicit that along the way. You have to be able to encourage the feedback, accept it, and then don't react to the feedback.

What I mean by not reacting is that you need to respond to it and do your best to improve yourself and your management style based on that feedback. But you can't retaliate against the individual who provides the feedback.

That's a hard thing to stomach as a manager. You have to be secure enough with your own abilities and skills to be able to accept that.

Now, not every piece of feedback will be accurate. Sometimes people will vent about something, and they just don't have all the information. So you have to take it with a grain of salt sometimes, especially when somebody's just mad in general.

But it's important to weigh every piece of feedback you get and ask yourself, "Was there something I said or something I did that caused this person to think this way about me?" And I found that nine times out of ten, you can think of a specific situation where maybe you didn't intend for this to happen. But this is how it was received. So I can understand that. So I need to work on that type of situation going forward.

The way to encourage that kind of feedback really comes down to building up that relationship of trust with each individual employee along the way. Ask for feedback frequently. And most of the time, they're going to be hesitant to give it to you right away. Or they'll give you a small softball piece of feedback. And then you just have to make sure you treat that with respect, so that they'll be more willing to give you bigger feedback along the way.

ACT ON THAT FEEDBACK

It's one thing to ask for feedback, but another altogether to demonstrate that you're willing to make those changes yourself. Doing that is one of the ways that Derek Mernagh, controller at Yelp, has been able to be an effective leader:

> *It's important to reach out to your team and have them assess your performance as a leader. Ask questions like, "What are the things that I could be doing more, to become a better leader?" If you don't listen to your chain, and if you don't show that you value their opinion, then they don't respect you as much as a leader. And I think if you reach out to them for feedback, just for the sake of feedback, they're going to see that too.*
>
> *So I think it's really important to get their insight, show that you're listening to their feedback, and act on it in a tangible way that they can see.*
>
> *I think you will not be an effective leader if you don't have the support and respect of your team. One of the key ways that I've been able to do that is through feedback.*

TECH TOOLS FOR GREATER ACCOUNTABILITY

Tech tools like FloQast introduce transparency, and transparency enables accountability. That's one thing that FloQast brings to the table. Our dashboard lets everyone see what tasks are assigned to which team member, who's getting stuff done, and who's the bottleneck. That can ruffle a lot of feathers when you make things more transparent. We find that the people who are resistant to FloQast are generally the ones who don't have a lot of work on their plate. They're being uncovered.

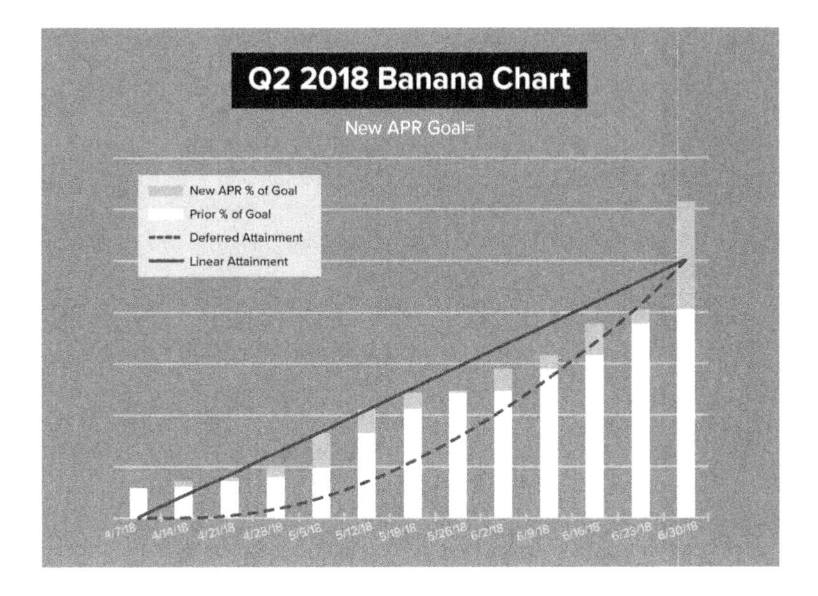

To stay on top of our sales goals at FloQast, I send out a "banana chart" to the whole company every week. This chart shows the recurring revenue we added during the previous week on top of the recurring revenue we've already made, and indicates the progress we're making towards our goals for the quarter. It's not a straight line, but rather curved like a banana, and gets steepest at the end of the quarter, when everything happens at once, and we (hopefully) hit our goal. Being transparent in this way incentivizes the whole company to work hard so that we achieve our sales goals. This same chart also goes out to our investors so that they see how we're doing on a consistent basis and aren't surprised by quarterly reports.

Accounting teams can do the same thing with the monthly close to accelerate performance and build a cohesive culture. This is why we added Close Analytics to FloQast. Like the banana chart we use to track sales at FloQast, this tracks the completion of tasks on a daily basis. Getting this chart to the

CFO every day eliminates the expectation gap, and keeps everyone accountable to getting the work done.

IS IT TIME TO DITCH THE ANNUAL PERFORMANCE REVIEW?

If your experience in accounting was like mine and many of my co-workers, you probably spent hours and hours filling out forms for annual performance reviews. While it is important to give and get feedback from your team, there are better ways of doing it.

Many organizations today are ditching the annual performance review, or adding more frequent, project-focused reviews. It doesn't make sense in today's agile companies to rate someone's performance just once a year, based on goals set months ago that have since become irrelevant.

While the annual review still has its place, getting feedback several times a year on an informal basis can help make sure everyone is hitting the standards they need to. Doing it only once a year doesn't work well for Millennials, and it doesn't work for the ways that companies are structured today.

Several chapters in the book *Nine Lies About Work* by Marcus Buckingham and Ashley Goodall discuss annual performance reviews. They conclude that no, people don't need feedback, they need attention, as I discussed earlier. And no, people can't reliably rate each other, but they can reliably rate their own experience. Buckingham and Goodall identified what they call the "Idiosyncratic Rater Effect." When they looked at the results of three large studies of how people rate each other, they found that "about 60% of the variability in ratings can be chalked up to the raters' differing responses to a rating scale."[4]

The Idiosyncratic Rater Effect means that there tends to be a higher correlation between the ratings that a particular rater assigns to the group they're rating than with the actual performance of a person as rated by a panel of raters. Each person doing the rating has a different notion of what "Exceeds Expectations" means. While Jane thinks that only two people in the group met that threshold, maybe Peter, looking at the same group, thinks that eight out of ten are at that level.

In a Harvard Business Review article that describes the development of a new performance review system at Deloitte, Buckingham and Goodall suggest that a better approach is asking team leaders four specific questions about their team members:[5]

1. Given what I know of this person's performance, and if it were my money, I would award this person the highest possible compensation increase and bonus [measures overall performance and unique value to the organization on a five-point scale from "strongly agree" to "strongly disagree"].
2. Given what I know of this person's performance, I would always want him or her on my team [measures ability to work well with others on the same five-point scale].
3. This person is at risk for low performance [identifies problems that might harm the customer or the team on a yes-or-no basis].
4. This person is ready for promotion today [measures potential on a yes-or-no basis].

These four questions bypass the subjective questions and zero in on the team leader's reaction to a particular team member. I especially like question 2, which really is the most important question to consider about members of your team.

CONSIDER AFTER-ACTION REVIEWS INSTEAD OF ANNUAL PERFORMANCE REVIEWS

After-action reviews or debriefs are a process the military uses to improve everyone's performance. This is how the Air Force Thunderbirds manage to teach pilots precision flying in just four months, with 50% turnover in the team each year. This is a method for extracting the lessons from experiences so that everyone learns and improves. It's a means of converting tribal knowledge into structural capital that everyone can use.

In an after-action review, a team sits down and discusses these questions:

1. What was supposed to happen?
2. What actually did happen?
3. What were the positive and negative factors?
4. What have we learned, and what can we do better next time?

To make an after-action review successful, everyone must agree that the information will not be used to blame, punish, or reward participants. Everyone needs to be candid about any mistakes they made. Most important, this information needs to be documented and made available as a learning tool for the entire organization so that the same mistakes aren't repeated, and so that the next iteration is better.

THE PEOPLE PROBLEM ISN'T GOING AWAY

Chances are it will get worse as Baby Boomers retire and the talent pool shrinks. But you can make it less of an issue by implementing the ideas in this section.

My best suggestion is to run a department you'd want to work in.

A consultant working with us summed up the culture of FloQast this way: "You guys are unapologetically Southern California, but you work your asses off." We come to work in shorts and T-shirts. I wear a hoodie instead of a suit jacket. It doesn't matter to us what you wear, just that you get the work done.

Cullen, Chris, and I have worked hard to create a workplace that has good people, is a great company, has great processes, is smart, works hard, yet is relaxed. And so many of the controllers and CFOs at our clients have done the same thing.

Creating a great **culture** will help you attract and retain the right **people**. **Trusting** those people to do their work effectively and efficiently will get you better results than micromanaging. Adding **accountability** on top encourages people to do their best and ensures that the work gets done.

But solving the challenge with people isn't the only challenge controllers have to deal with. There's a whole world of risk out there.

Our job as accountants in the new world of real-time technology, is to effectively anticipate and mitigate those risks.

PART 3

TAMING RISK WITH TECH

8 / CHALLENGES WITH RISK

A lot of times people look at risk and ask, 'What are the odds that I will succeed?' A different way to look at risk is to ask, 'What's the worst thing that would happen if I failed?

–Dave Hitz

When you live in Southern California, you're bound to run into surfers. You might even take up the sport. One of the first lessons you learn is that the secret to catching the best wave is anticipating where the wave will be. Just being agile isn't enough. You have to be in the right place at the right time, moving at the right speed. If you wait until you see where the wave crests, it's too late.

Unlike surfers, we accountants have only looked backwards. We've only paid attention to where the waves were. That's what GAAP teaches us to do. And for most of us, learning GAAP and understanding FASB pronouncements was the bulk of our accounting education.

Until recently, looking backwards served us well. Due to the previous limits of information technology, compiling past results was really all we could do. But today's technology is pulling that visible line of past results closer and closer to the present. Instead of waiting weeks or days to see numbers, automation means we don't have to wait for someone to key in the numbers. Transactions can enter the system almost in real time. Soon all reporting will be in real time, or close to it.

That means that finance professionals have to switch their perspective from the rear view mirror to the front windshield. GAAP is the rear view mirror. The future is the front windshield, and is a whole lot bigger than the rear view mirror. Accountants need to be looking ahead, to anticipate where the waves will be, and where the biggest risks to our companies — and our careers — will be.

REDUCE RISK BY ANTICIPATING THE FUTURE

Back in 1998, Sergey Brin and Larry Page wanted to go back to school, so they offered their little search engine company Google up for sale for a cool $1 million. Alta Vista, Yahoo,[1] and Excite[2] all turned them down. Today, Yahoo still exists, but who even remembers Alta Vista or Excite?

When Apple first introduced the iPhone in 2007, Jim Balsillie, co-CEO of Research in Motion (RIM), maker of the Blackberry, told his panicky co-CEO Mike Lazaridis, "We'll be fine."[3] Balsillie could not envision a future where the Blackberry would become irrelevant.

If the leaders of RIM, Alta Vista or Excite had been able to peer into the future, think how different those companies would be today. Predicting the future is impossible, right? But futurist Daniel Burrus has developed a way of looking at what's happening today, and leveraging that to predict what the future is likely to be.

In 2017, he published *The Anticipatory Organization: Turn Disruption and Change into Opportunity and Advantage.* This book, by the way, should be mandatory reading for modern controllers or anyone who doesn't want to be left behind by the accelerating changes of the modern world. He even teamed up with the Maryland Association of CPAs to put together a course specifically for accountants and finance professionals, which you can learn about at macpa.org.

According to Burrus, "We are living in a time of accelerating digital disruption—not mere change, but game-changing, transformational change." And the pace of change is never going to be slower than it is now. Those waves are coming faster and faster, so we've got to fine-tune our predictive skills.

The key, as Burrus explains in the book, is learning to predict the future by developing an anticipatory mindset. This mindset will allow you to identify the trends that will lead to opportunities that your competitors will miss.

Burrus differentiates between "hard trends" and "soft trends." Hard trends are trends that we know will occur. For example, we know that the Boomer generation is getting older and that most of them will retire soon, if they haven't already. We know that the use of cloud technology will continue to increase. And we know that the accounting, tax, and other regulations we have to follow will only become more complex. These are things we can count on in the future.

Another hard trend is that technology will continue to evolve rapidly. Already technology advances have made it easier to collect, summarize, disseminate, and analyze data about the performance of our organizations. Those improvements to our financial systems, combined with the rapid pace of today's world means that the job of the controller is becoming more complex and data-driven.

A soft trend is something that might happen. Soft trends are things that can be influenced, but the outcome is not yet certain.They're based on assumptions about what might happen in the future, not on verifiable facts. For example, Facebook is the dominant social media platform today, but leadership issues or a new upstart platform could challenge that in the future.

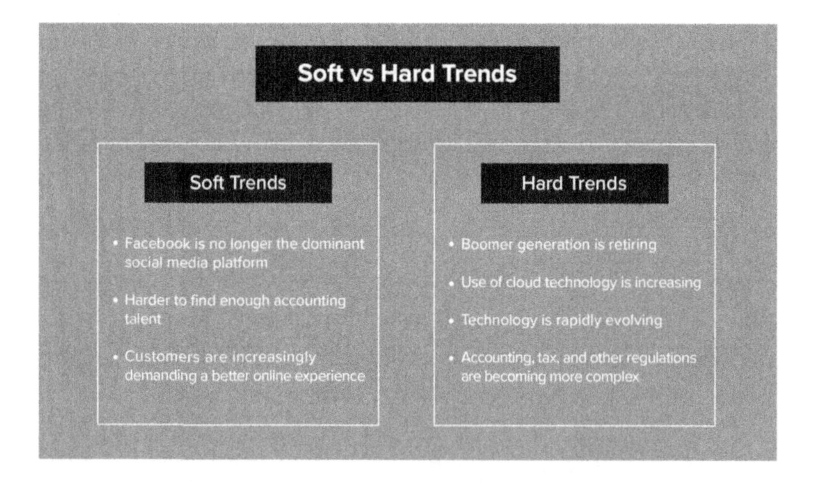

An example of a soft trend impacting finance is that it will be harder to find enough accounting talent to get the work done. But this trend can be influenced, at least in how it impacts your organization, as we discussed at length in Part II of this book. We can work on creating a place where people want to work, so we'll never have a shortage of qualified applicants. And, as I'll discuss in this section, we can leverage technology so that we don't need as many people to get the work done.

Another soft trend is that customers are increasingly demanding a better online experience with everyone they do business with. Your company website needs to be easy to use with clear navigation and plenty of free and useful information. It should be easy for people to find what they want, and convenient for them to do business with you online.

If you take the time to think about hard and soft trends, and try to imagine how they might interact in the future, you may come up with opportunities that no one else has even thought about. This can also help you avoid future risks that could damage your company or your career.

WHAT WILL YOUR COMPANY LOOK LIKE IN A YEAR?

One exercise I recommend to force this kind of visionary and anticipatory thinking is to sit down on your own and think about each department within the company. Write down a few notes for each department about what they look like today. Then think about what they're going to look like at the end of next year. Think in terms of hiring, what types of technology they might implement, and what are the risks. Consider the risks that are already there and how things will evolve. What will change? Where might there be risk intersections that you can do something about today?

Going through this exercise on a regular basis, and then looking back at your own projections will help you learn to be more of an anticipatory thinker.

TEAM UP WITH FP&A

Consider also sitting down with your FP&A person to talk about the projections for next year and what the growth pattern looks like. Ask that person what they think about the things you're noticing. Ideally, what you want to aim for is not just relying on your FP&A person to keep you updated on what the plans are across the different departments, but you want to be sitting in those meetings with marketing and sales and all the others. That way, you're in a position to act on what you hear firsthand.

Sometimes accounting and FP&A have a more adversarial relationship. That's because they have different perspectives on the numbers. GAAP is backward-looking, while FP&A looks to the future. FP&A uses the numbers from accounting as a starting point, and combines that with external research. But if the journal entries aren't booked correctly, or if there are other issues with the data from accounting, then the projections and forecasts from FP&A won't be accurate.

So instead I recommend having an open relationship. Acknowledging to your FP&A person that GAAP, and especially all the craziness with revenue recognition, leases, and CECL, are based on a lot of estimates and professional judgment can go a long way towards creating a better relationship. Also, asking your FP&A person what they need to do their job better can turn conflict into cooperation. Remember, you're both on the same team, doing the best you can to help your organization be successful.

THE ROLE OF THE CONTROLLER IS CHANGING

As our survey[4] pointed out, the role of the controller is changing to become more strategic. With the rapid pace of change in our world and in your business, everyone needs to see what's happening now, not what happened three weeks or three months ago. CEOs need CFOs who are more business partners than historians. That means that CFOs are taking on more board-level strategy, which used to be the domain of the CEO. They're also taking on part of the COO, CIO, and

CHR responsibilities, so the work they used to do is getting pushed down to controllers.

Modern controllers who want to leverage this hard trend are looking for ways to expand their strategic role in their organization. They aren't just closing the books and getting reports to the CFO. They're taking on jobs that the CFOs or CIOs used to do.

Here's an example of a modern controller, from an article in the Wall Street Journal:[5] Heather Dixon, corporate controller and chief accounting officer at health insurer Aetna Inc., oversees the company's tax and finance shared-services group. She also took on a leadership role in Aetna's combination with CVS Health Corp.

We saw this in our survey of accounting and finance professionals,[6] where 95% of the 306 survey respondents said that the role of the controller was becoming more strategic than it was just a decade ago. Most controllers (90%) reported spending more time on strategic planning than they did ten years ago. Risk management and mitigation, and talent management are other areas where controllers are spending significantly more time today than in the past.

A recent survey by Deloitte and the IMA[7] found three distinct categories of controllers, based on the amount of time they spent on traditional versus strategic functions. A free, on-demand webcast by Deloitte[8] also discusses the transformation of the controller's role. In Deloitte's taxonomy, the traditional functions of controllers encompass the **stewardship** role of managing risk and preserving assets, and the **operations** role of running an efficient finance operation. The traditional role includes things like internal control and having a clean audit. Strategic tasks — which will become a bigger part of the controller's work in the future — include providing strategic insights, overseeing the digital transformation of finance operations and taking on more responsibility for the complex business and regulatory environments.

Traditional controllers said they spend 75-100% of their time on the activities of the traditional role. But strategic controllers spend less than 60% of time doing the traditional activities. Some spend no time at all. In between those extremes are what Deloitte labeled the mixed persona.

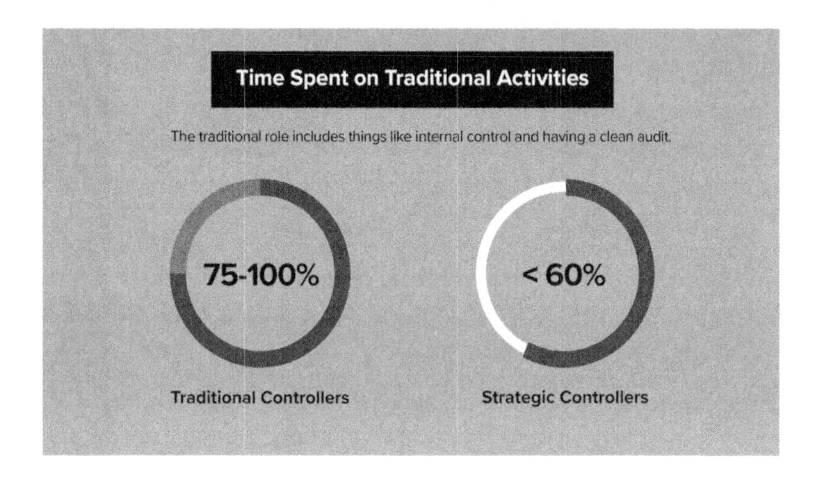

However much — or little — time controllers spend on the traditional functions, most controllers would prefer to spend less time on those kinds of tasks. Most would rather increase the amount of time they have for strategic functions. However, because they are still required to make sure all the compliance and reporting is done, they may not have the time or energy to do the strategic work. Finding the time, energy, and resources to improve their skills can also be a struggle, which can lead to a lack of confidence to raise their hand when the opportunity arises.

With all of these pressures, it's not surprising that 89% of the finance pros we surveyed[9] said that the job of controller was getting more stressful.

The good thing about the work being pushed down is that for controllers with an eye on moving to the CFO position, all these extra responsibilities give them the opportunity to learn some of the skills they'll need to be great CFOs.

These changes to the controller's role have been happening for a while. Although our survey found that the role of the controller has changed significantly in the last ten years, a 2008 research report by EY[10] found that "eight out of ten FCs [financial controllers] say their job has become more challenging in the last five years, while only 5% consider it to have become less challenging."

This is consistent with the observations of Richard Susskind and Daniel Susskind in their book, *The Future of the Professions.* Across all professions — not just accounting and finance — they observed that the users of professional services have been under tremendous cost pressure. Everyone wants professional services that are more in-depth and more complex, but they also want to pay less for those services. The Susskinds first observed this trend in their research and in their work with clients in 2004 and 2005. Since the 2008 recession, the "less-for-more" challenge has only accelerated.

As technology drives changes across all parts of every business, finance teams will no longer be an isolated silo within a business, but will become interwoven into all parts of the business. This will require controllers and their teams to communicate better with everyone in the company as well as the board and investors. Accountants will have to become better communicators of financial information to non-accountants.

These changes across business and the finance function mean that as controllers take on more responsibilities, they will have to also embrace risk. And the risks controllers will have to consider aren't only those that impact the finance department. Those are the ones we see if we're focused exclusively in the rear-view mirror. Controllers will have to play a bigger game. We have to be looking forward, and expand our vision to see the bigger view out the front windshield.

Many of us got our start in accounting as auditors, where we learned to make decisions based on risk. Those risk assessments came from the best available information we had. Today, we're awash in a sea of information. So much information that it's hard to decide what information is most useful or valuable to us. If we're not paying attention, it's easy to miss risks that can lead to opportunities or to disasters, depending on how we respond.

When I was growing up, there was a video rental store on just about every corner. The biggest of them all was Blockbuster. They had thousands of stores across the country and around the world, and millions of customers. But their dirty secret was that a big chunk of their revenue came from late fees, which customers hated.

Along came Netflix, with a completely different business model: customers would subscribe, and could watch as many movies as they wanted, and keep those movies for days or weeks without any late fees. That completely disrupted the video rental business model, which is now pretty much gone. Blockbuster declared bankruptcy in 2010, and today, from those thousands of stores around the world, there's just one Blockbuster store left.[11]

WHAT ARE THE BIGGEST RISKS TODAY?

The biggest risks this year may be the ones that barely registered last year. That's why I was glad to come across this annual survey by Protiviti and North Carolina State University of the biggest risks for 2019. Since 2013, these two organizations have been asking C-suite executives and directors around the world what they see as the biggest risks for the coming year. Here's what those respondents said would be the top 10 risks facing businesses in 2019:[12]

1. **Existing operations and infrastructure unable to adjust to competitors from "born digital" firms.** By this point in the book, you should understand why technology is essential to the finance function of your organization. But have you considered how risky it could be for your whole organization if it doesn't stay on the leading edge? Digital business models are springing up all over that have qualities that legacy companies lack: they tend to have low barriers to entry, they're easy to scale, and they can respond quickly to changing market conditions, all qualities that legacy companies lack. Many of our clients — and FloQast itself — are eager participants in this new digital world.
2. **Succession challenges and ability to attract and retain top talent.** Companies struggling with their digital infrastructure get a double whammy here: the short supply of the best and brightest of the younger generation aren't interested in working for organizations that aren't digital ready or companies that don't reflect their values. Mature companies may struggle to hire and retain young team members if they're not innovative enough for the younger generations.
3. **Regulatory changes and regulatory scrutiny.** FASB threw us a curveball by making us implement the new revenue recognition and lease accounting standards at the same time. The Supreme Court's Wayfair decision opened the possibility for states to charge sales tax on internet sales. Plus, depending on your industry and where your company does

business, states and local governments are always throwing new rules at us. California, where FloQast is located, has more regulations than any other state. And if you do business overseas, there's GDPR and Brexit to worry about. Add in some political gridlock, and it's almost impossible to predict what we'll have to comply with next.

4. **Managing cyber threats.** Some say there are two types of companies today: those who have had their security breached and know about it, and those who have had their security breached and don't know about it. Digital transformation, cloud computing, AI, mobile usage, and the exponential increases to computing power, bandwidth, and computing storage are moving faster than our ability to secure our data and our infrastructure from cyber attacks. Those attacks are becoming increasingly sophisticated, so we need to be ever more vigilant.
5. **Resistance to change.** The pace of change we have now is the slowest it will ever be in the future. Organizations and individuals within our organizations who are unwilling to let go of the old ways of doing business out of fear of the unknown run the risk of becoming dinosaurs. If you're old enough, you might remember that the CEO of RIM, the maker of the Blackberry, doubted that anyone would ever want to watch video on a phone when the first iPhone came out.
6. **Rapid speed of disruptive innovations and new technologies.** Your organization — and most likely many of the jobs within your organization — will be disrupted at some point by technological innovation. If we look to history as a model, new technologies tend to raise the bar for what customers

expect from us. Companies that don't adapt to those new expectations risk losing market share.

7. **Privacy/identity management and information security.** The very advances in technology that allow us to harness the power of big data and collect relevant data about our customers make us inviting to crooks who want to use that information for their own benefit. Tech companies are also at risk of losing proprietary pieces of their business to online theft.
8. **Inability to utilize analytics and big data.** Inexpensive data storage means we've got an ocean of data about our customers, our markets, and our operations. The vastness of that data means it's beyond humans relying on Excel alone to extract useful insights in the time frame that we need that information. If we can't leverage the data that's out there, our competitors will.
9. **An organization's culture may not sufficiently encourage timely identification and escalation of risk issues.** Top-down management and rigid channels of communication can make it nearly impossible to address new problems coming in from the front lines. There's no expedient way to get that information to the decision makers when it has to go through layers and layers of middle managers. The old suggestion box won't hack it anymore. Complacency and an attitude of "that's how we've always done it" leaves an organization open to becoming irrelevant.
10. **Sustaining customer loyalty and retention.** Customers have access to more information about their problems and the solutions offered by our products and services, and those of our competitors, than ever. If we're not proactive in solving their

> current problems better — and identifying and solving the problems they may not yet realize they have — they'll defect to our competitors. The ease of changing vendors — which makes it easy for new customers to pick us — also makes it easy for them to ditch us.

SO HOW WELL ARE COMPANIES HANDLING RISK?

You have to be an ostrich with your head in the sand if you're not aware of the risks I listed above. For 10 years, the AICPA and the Enterprise Risk Management Initiative at NC State's Poole College of Management have been surveying CFOs, controllers, and other senior finance leaders who are also members of the AICPA's Business and Industry group about their organizations' approaches to risk management. The latest survey,[13] performed in the fall of 2018, shows that there's a disconnect between the magnitude of the risks faced by organizations and their approaches to managing those risks.

While more than half (59%) of respondents believe that the number and complexity of risks is increasing over time, only about 3% of those organizations feel their organizations have a robust strategy in place to manage risk. At the same time, exactly half of the respondents say their organization's culture is risk averse.

So even though everyone knows that risk is increasing, and they say they're risk averse, there's little being done to manage that risk.

What's more troubling is that more than half (57%) said that risk management doesn't play a big role in strategic planning. According to the study's authors, "A better understanding of risks facing the organization should provide rich input to the strategic planning process so that management and the board can design strategic goals and initiatives with those risks in mind." Even though the survey indicated that the "majority of organizations appear to be fairly unstructured, casual, and somewhat ad hoc in how they identify, assess, and monitor key risk exposures, responses to several questions indicate a high level of confidence that risks are being strategically managed in an effective manner." About half of respondents believed that risks were being monitored in some way besides through enterprise risk management.

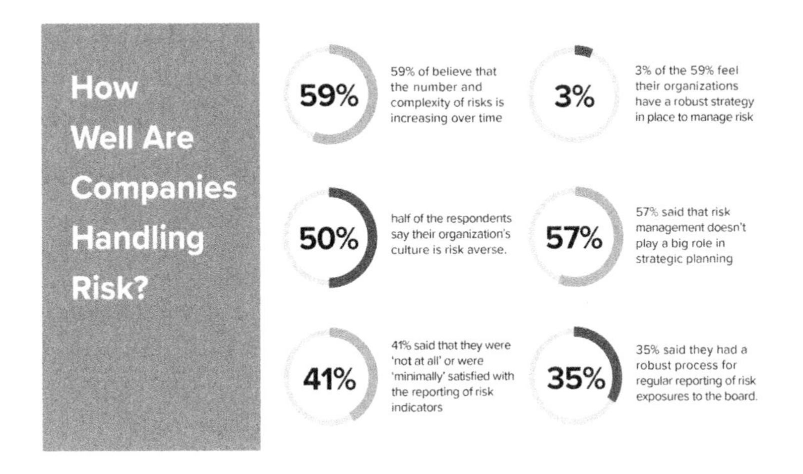

If there aren't robust methods for managing and monitoring current risks, what exactly are the processes that provide organization leaders and boards a clear view into the risks on the horizon?

Maybe part of the problem is that many organizations don't have any systematic methods for communicating about risk. According to the survey, "almost half (41%) of our respondents admitted that they were 'not at all' or were 'minimally' satisfied with the nature and extent of the internal reporting of key risk indicators (known as KRIs) to senior executives."

So executives are aware that they don't know what's out there, and because they don't know what's out there, they're blindly relying on the "unstructured, casual, and somewhat ad hoc" methods their organizations are using to monitor risk.

Even though the survey found that boards and other external stakeholders are asking for more information about how organizations are handling risk, only 35% of respondents said they had a systematic and robust process for regular reporting of risk exposures to the board.

The best explanation I can come up with for the paradoxical results from this survey is that many leaders really do have their heads buried in the sand, and are in denial about the reality of the risks they're facing.

I admit that many of the risks that companies will face in the future are out of the purview of finance leaders. But someone needs to be looking ahead. Demonstrating anticipatory thinking can help make you a leader in your company.

Maybe it's because we've still got that startup vibe here at FloQast, but we're always looking at what's ahead. We always keep our eyes on what the competition is doing, and thanks to team members who have their fingers firmly on the pulse of the future of accounting technology, we are planning for the future. That's one reason we're adding additional services like Flux Analysis and AutoRec, so that when — and not if, but **when** — continuous accounting becomes the norm, we'll have lots to offer when the month-end close becomes a one-click close.

ACCOUNTING AND FINANCE ARE THE SWITZERLAND OF THE BUSINESS

Risk is admittedly really broad. There's the risk of failing your audit. The risk of losing compliance around your SOC report. The risk of fraud — are people going to be stealing money from us? Are we going to go out of business because we're burning cash and no one knows how to spend appropriately?

But what's cool is accounting can help with every kind of risk. Accounting and finance can switch up their mentality from bean counters and become more like business-wide consultants. They can take a Switzerland approach, where you're not allied with any one department, but what you want is what's best for the company as a whole, regardless of how that happens. Your position in the company gives you a certain amount of independence.

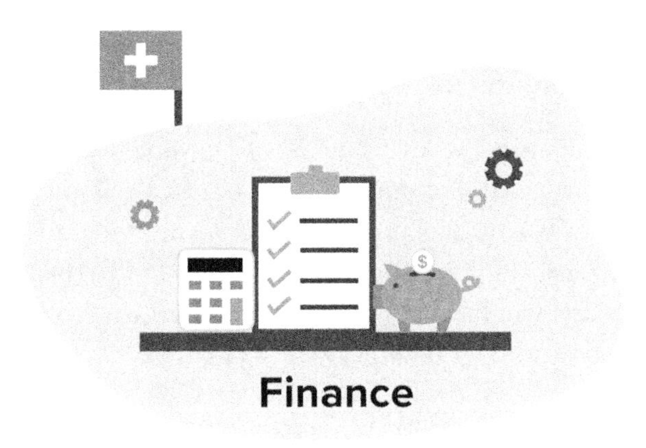

For a long time, accounting and finance have been the bad guys who say no because of the budget. And now that bad guy persona is percolating down into processes as well. To mitigate risk, controllers are putting in technology and processes that might be perceived as extra work that people in other departments maybe don't want to do. For example, over in engineering here at FloQast, I have to get numbers for capitalized software. And I have to tell people that from a compliance point of view, this person can't approve certain lines of code because it would ruin our SOC reporting compliance.

But instead of having that bad guy persona, the controller is in the position to take the Switzerland approach, a neutral stance. To be more of an independent consultant whose interest is always on what's best overall for the company. As that independent, neutral party, I can go to engineering and explain to them why we need to do this as a way to mitigate risk.

It's a mindset shift. It's from being the bad cop to being an enabler for the company. You can really shift the conversation by going into it with the attitude of "how can I help this business get better?" Controllers have the ability to be more like a consultant to every part of the business. What you can offer is insight into the organization as a whole from a neutral center that only wants the business to do well.

Because you are an advocate for the whole company, and because as a controller you can interface with all parts of the company, you can also point out when the different parts of the company aren't aligned in strategy. From that neutral center where you have the purview of the entire company, you can be a powerful consultant to each department.

Being a consultant to each department doesn't mean going into meetings and trying to make the other person happier. Sometimes that's just not going to happen, especially when you want them to do something that seems like extra work, like putting in extra controls. But you've got to think at a higher level and do what's best for the company.

That kind of work — keeping all the departments aligned and headed in the same direction — used to be the CFO's job. But with more work being pushed down, the modern controller has to step up their game to be an advocate for the whole company.

WHAT TO DO ABOUT RISK?

Risk won't go away if we ignore it, and if you're like me, that list above likely made you squirm. One of the big themes in that list is technology.

- Digital businesses are threatening legacy brick and mortar organizations.
- Talent won't stick around if you're using old technology.
- Our increasingly digitized workplace makes us vulnerable to cyber attacks in ways that paper and file cabinets were not.
- Technology will disrupt the ways we work and do business.
- Without technology as a tool to understand our data, we're losing out on potential valuable insights.

As you recall, our formula for technology is as follows:

Technology = Process + Tools + Knowledge

I can't promise that if you strengthen all the elements in that equation, you'll be safe from risk, but you'll at least be better off than your competitors who don't. And I admit that controllers might not have a lot of ability to influence the risk situation at their organizations. But if you want to move from the traditional role to a strategic role, you'll need to start thinking about how you can reduce risk in your organization. So let's take a look at how each of these elements can help you solve the risk problem.

9 / IMPLEMENT ALL THE TECH YOU CAN

Any sufficiently advanced technology is indistinguishable from magic.
–Arthur C. Clarke

The amazing thing about being in accounting today is all the technology we have at our disposal. Tech that pulls information from different sources and records it in our ERP. Tech to help reconcile accounts. Tech that extracts data from our ERP and combines it with other information from our CRM to create reports that help the sales team focus their energies on the most profitable kinds of prospects.

And this is just the beginning. If future tech developments follow the same path we've seen in the past decade, remarkable things will happen. Here are just a few to think about:

- **Tech is getting smaller.** Ask your Baby Boomer colleagues what the first cell phones were like — big, bulky, and with crappy sound. Now you've got a super computer in your pocket.
- **Mobile is the future.** Cell phones, tablets, laptops, and wifi everywhere mean you're not tied to a desktop computer in an office to get work done. Besides reading and responding to email, search is moving to mobile. In the third quarter of 2013, just 27% of search was done on a mobile device. By the first quarter of 2019, mobile moved up to 59% of search.[1]
- **Everything talks to everything else.** Sensors in new cars alert when you're too close to the one in front. Soon, warehouse sensors will notice when it's time to reorder and will automatically order more.

CHANGES IN TECH ARE ACCELERATING

Like it or not, technology is advancing faster than you can blink. What was new yesterday may be obsolete in just a few years. A large part of this is due to Moore's Law, which was proposed by George Moore, co-founder of Intel, back in 1965, and it's still holding true today. Moore's Law says that processing power in microchips doubles about every two years. Over the same time frame, the price drops by about half.

Moore's law means that in two years, we'll be able to do things with technology that aren't possible now, things that might seem like a fantasy today. Think of Siri for business. Imagine being able to pull up an app on your tablet or phone and asking for the latest sales figures.

Sound impossible? BQE Software (bqe.com) just introduced Core Intelligence, which allows users to do just that with BQE's GL. Intuit has a version of that for QuickBooks, which was debuted at QuickBooks Connect in San Jose in 2017. Intuit's version is still in beta status, but we'll see more apps like that in the future.

Review Note: Exponential change and technology

Futurist and Google chief engineer Ray Kurzweil uses the following folk tale to explain the rate of exponential change:

> *According to legend, the inventor of chess demonstrated his new game to an ancient emperor of China. The emperor was so enchanted with the game that he told the inventor to name anything he wanted as a reward. The inventor said that his desires were simple, so he wanted to be paid in rice. He asked for one grain of rice to be placed on the first square of the chessboard, two grains on the second, four on the third, eight on the fourth, and so on, doubling each time, all the way to the 64th square.*
>
> *The emperor agreed, thinking he had made a good bargain, and that this would amount to just a few large bags of rice.*
>
> *For the first few squares, this seems reasonable. But by the 32nd square, this is more than two billion grains of rice, about what you might harvest from a field. And when you get to the second half of the chessboard, the numbers get really big, really fast. If this process continues to the end, you'll have a pile of rice bigger than Mt. Everest.*
>
> *So as the exponential growth of the piles of rice continued, the emperor saw he had been swindled. Being emperor, he simply had the inventor executed.*

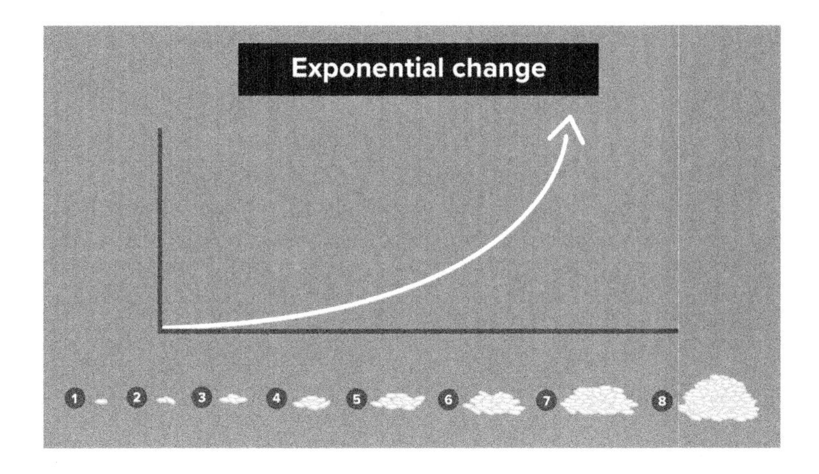

If we assume that Moore's Law will continue to be true — and it has so far — Kurzweil contends that we are in the "second half of the chessboard" with technological change.[2]

This means that the pace of change is only going to accelerate. If you're not already implementing as much technology as you can, you're only going to be left further behind.

THE THREE DIGITAL ACCELERATORS

As Burrus describes in *The Anticipatory Organization,* we've got three powerful digital accelerators that will propel technology changes into exponential growth.

1. **Computing Power.** Today's smartphones are more powerful than all of NASA's computing power in 1969, combined.[3] And, thanks to cloud technology, we're less dependent on the machines in our desktops since we're using them to access supercomputers.
2. **Bandwidth.** Some of you might be old enough to

remember the early days of dial-up access to the internet, when downloading large documents took hours. Today, we can download a spreadsheet or a book to our phone in seconds.

3. **Digital Storage.** The first computers had no hard drives. Files couldn't be larger than the capacity of a floppy disk, which was a puny 160 kilobytes. Today, hard drives are measured in terabytes. And with cloud computing, we have access to as much storage space as we want.

These three digital accelerators mean that tech of tomorrow will make the hottest things of today look primitive by comparison. The biggest way tech is impacting accountants today is by automation, which wasn't possible until these three accelerators opened the door.

AUTOMATION LETS ACCOUNTANTS BE ACCOUNTANTS

For centuries, accounting was done laboriously by hand by recording entries in journals, adding them up, and transferring them to a general ledger. Then we got computers, which essentially reproduced what accountants did by hand in an electronic format. But it didn't change the fundamental nature of the work.

Now with AI, RPA, blockchain, machine learning, and cognitive computing, we have the opportunity for real innovation. These technologies have the potential to completely transform the nature of how we do our work and how the product of our work is used by others.

Automation creates bandwidth so controllers aren't stuck in the weeds. As technology allows us to move closer to real time reporting, our organizations will rely less on periodic reporting and more on self-service dashboards.

Technology is helping everyone serve their customers better. For controllers, your customers include everyone in the organization:

- The CEO and the board, who rely on the information from the CFO to make decisions.
- The CFO, who relies on the information you provide to understand what's going on in the organization.
- Marketing, who needs your help to figure out which campaigns are winners and which to abandon.
- Sales, who needs to know what kinds of prospects make the most profitable and enduring customers.
- Operations, who needs to know when costs deviate from budget.

To serve his or her customers well, the modern controller needs to have their finger on the pulse of the organization.

Review Note - Automation helps smaller companies fight fraud

Smaller companies don't typically have the kinds of internal controls that the larger ones have to implement thanks to Sarbanes Oxley. But automation helps controllers and their teams pick up their heads and think about things a little differently, as opposed to just getting through the close and moving on to the next one.

They have bandwidth to think about what kinds of fraud can happen and figure out some controls to put in place. For example, making sure that fake vendors aren't being created so that someone's being paid improperly. Or that you don't have fake employees, or that valuable inventory isn't walking out the door. At really small companies, even just making sure that the owner looks over bank statements and credit card statements can go a long way towards mitigating risk.

THE CLOUD IS HERE

Cloud technology makes it easier — and more affordable — to upgrade a legacy ERP to a cloud ERP. As a measure of the spread of cloud technology, in the first quarter of 2019, spending on software surpassed IT infrastructure for the first time in US history.[4]

So I'm assuming that if you're reading this book, you're already sold on cloud technology, and if you're not already using a cloud ERP, you're putting together a game plan to make it happen. I won't go into too many details of the advantages, but here are a few, in brief:

- **Greater flexibility**. Cloud ERPs let you work the way your company works. Employees can work wherever they want, using almost any device they want.
- **Lower maintenance costs**. No more expensive servers to buy and maintain because everything is stored in the cloud. With the SaaS model, your initial investment is much less, and you always have access to the latest version update.
- **Better security**. Cloud providers are always upgrading to defend against the latest threats, and their facilities have the kinds of biometric, state-of-the-art security defenses you can only dream about.
- **Better customer service**. Today's cloud ERPs integrate with tools that make it easier for customers to interact with you.

Being on the leading edge of the tech revolution isn't just about making the accounting department more efficient. Research by McKinsey shows that the most aggressive adopters of AI and automation are more profitable than their peers.[5]

By automating as much as possible, you won't need as many people to do the work. For example, Intacct plus Salesforce and one person could conceivably replace a six-person billing department.

Companies that invest heavily in technology and automation have an easier time finding the right people, according to McKinsey:

> The most advanced adopters of AI and automation will also have an advantage when it comes to hiring, as they will tend to attract talent and can offer higher wages, if they successfully reap the productivity and performance gains from the technology adoption. They will have the freedom of choice to hire, as well as potentially contracting or retraining as suits their approach to ensuring that they have the relevant skills they need.[6]

Having technology in place gives your company advantages in hiring. First, you need fewer people to do the work. In a tight job market, this means you can actually hire the appropriate number of people. And if your headcount is lower, you might be able to pay them more, which always helps with retention.

Second, you have an easier time attracting the right people because tech makes the job more fun. There's less tedious, boring data entry, and more time to think. One of my CPA friends told me a horror story about being hired in audit at a small firm with almost no tech. She was basically tied to her desk, keying in endless trial balance after trial balance. She wasn't even allowed to run across the street to grab a bite for lunch. She was expected to bring food with her and eat at her desk. Not surprisingly, she left that place after two months.

Plus, technology helps your people do more interesting work, as Product Manager Erika Hecksher reminded me:

> *Something else to keep in mind is that people who go into this work seldom if ever get to do the interesting work that they learn about when they are getting their degrees. They are mostly just compiling data and doing the same thing over and over. We can help them get to the interesting work with technology.*

According to our survey, 67% of high-growth companies said they were implementing modern technology to solve hiring problems, so this isn't the future. Tech is helping companies keep their headcount down.

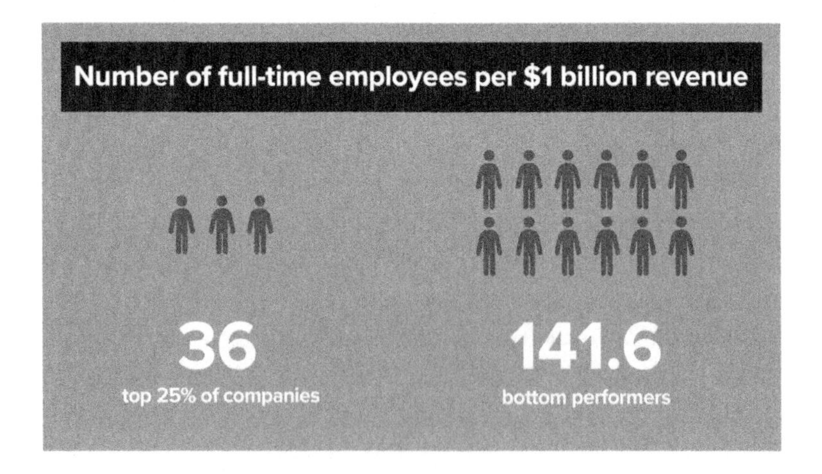

A recent article on CFO.com[7] looked at the number of full-time employees in finance per $1 billion in revenue. Their top 25% of companies averaged 36 FTEs per $1 billion, compared to the bottom performers who needed 141.6 per $1

billion. Accounting staff at the bottom performers were more likely to spend their time processing and entering transactions, while those at the top had more time and brain power for strategic thinking.

BUILD A TECH STACK THAT PRODUCES A SINGLE SOURCE OF TRUTH

More and more, IT is reporting into the finance function. With automation and a tech stack that works together, you're ensuring accuracy and creating efficiencies that will help you big time in the long run. This creates a single source of truth for the company that other departments can rely on.

A benefit of cloud-based ERPs is that they tend to be modular so the base system doesn't need to perform every single function you need it to. There's always the 20% that will be unique to your organization that will be a challenge. Building your tech stack means you work closely with IT, and you monitor it regularly to make sure that the connections don't break and that it's working the way it should.

Of course, the best reason to build a tech stack that works together is leveraging the power of automation. Automation saves you and your team time and reduces errors. Fewer errors means reconciliation is easier. Fewer errors also gives the FP&A folks a starting point they can trust.

TECH WILL HELP YOU ATTRACT AND RETAIN THE BEST PEOPLE

Updating your workplace tech not only helps your people do their work better and gives your company access to better information, it can also improve your company's ability to attract and retain talent. According to a Harvard Business Review study, 58% of the respondents said that job candidates consider a potential employer's technology and devices when deciding where to work.[8] Even if you get the talent, 51% of respondents said that outdated technology was making it hard to retain their best people.

Those responses echo what we found in our survey of 506 accounting and finance professionals.[9] Among our survey respondents, investing in technology was the most important way that companies were attracting and retaining talent. Over half (53%) said they were implementing modern technology such as cloud and mobile tech to help their teams improve efficiency, and 49% were providing technology to allow remote work. According to our survey, 86% of Millennials expect that technology will make our work more interesting.

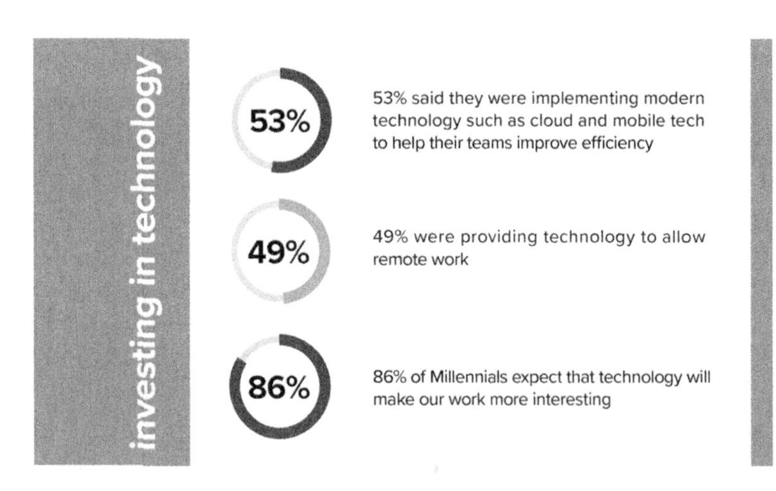

The return on your investment in software and people comes from being able to attract and retain the best talent, and get more work done in less time, and maybe even with fewer people. That time savings frees them up to focus on more strategic projects that can make the business better, to be the Switzerland of the company. This also sets your CFO up for success when they report to the board.

THE BIGGEST ENEMY IS THE STATUS QUO

Throughout the accounting world, technology is transforming what accountants do. In public accounting firms, automation is leading to the commoditization of tax and audit, which is driving prices down. Some firms are scrambling to find new ways to provide value to clients while others will simply die as their partners retire.

Many accountants in industry think that the way they've done the work for years or decades is simply the way that the work is done, and see no need to change. But as we've all seen, complacency can lead to errors, or missing something that could have been addressed when it was small but has now blown up.

Our Director of Sales Operations, Shivang Patel, told me about a sales training he went to recently, where the trainer talked about the two kinds of reasons people do things — a positive reinforcement or a negative aversion, a reward or solving a pain point. The trainer put it in these terms: "You're chasing a gold medal or you're running away from a German Shepherd."

To those who are trapped in the status quo, Shivang has this to say:

> *They don't know that a German Shepard exists. And they don't know that there's a gold medal out there for them to get. They're just comfortable right here, and that's the status quo. But it's always so rewarding when we speak to customers after they've implemented FloQast who say 'this has changed my life', 'this has shaved three days off our close', or 'my team is happier, they're leaving at five and not ten at night anymore' — these are all beautiful things to hear.*

FloQast co-founder and CTO, Cullen Zandstra, talks about using technology as a "starting point of regaining one's life." Technology can remove some of the chaos that controllers must manage. By using technology to keep track of tasks, and to send out alerts when something is out of balance, controllers can spend less time multitasking and context switching, and more time focusing "on the things that humans are really good at," as Cullen says.

The ones who aren't stuck in the status quo are the younger employees who see that technology means there's a better way to do their job. They're not as averse to new technology. They're willing to try something out because they try a new app on their phone every week.

It's this gift of technology that can empower accountants to do things in a different way. Millennials have seized on this as a way to do their jobs and manage their lives better. Older generations might not have had the self-confidence to question why we were doing something a certain way, or to question the SALY mentality, or to change the way they did their work. But now, technology and the way that Millennials embrace it is opening the door for all generations to push against the status quo, and to create ways for accountants to be more strategic in their jobs and their careers.

KEEP UP OR RISK BEING LEFT BEHIND

A 2019 report by the AICPA, CIMA, and Oracle identified a subset of finance leaders that they called Digital Finance Leaders.[10] According to the report, these finance leaders exhibit these characteristics:

- They have **implemented robotic process automation** at scale, focusing on automation of transactional tasks such as record-to-report.
- They prioritize the **re-engineering of legacy finance processes** to transform finance efficiency.
- They have driven scalable deployment of **advanced analytics tools** across the finance function**.**
- They have a clear view of **what data has the greatest value** to their organization and which has the least value.
- They play a **significant and influential role** in partnering with other lines of business to help improve decision making and performance management.
- They are **widely recognized by business stakeholders** for displaying commercial acumen and business understanding.

Perhaps not coincidentally, the organizations that these Digital Finance Leaders belong to tend to be highly digital themselves: 86% said their organizations have a "digital-first and cloud-first mindset," and 85% said their organizations have created a compelling digital customer experience. The approach of these organizations to technology for accounting operations has shifted from *cost reduction* to *investment.*

These companies aren't worried about digital disruption. They intend to be the disruptors.

But before you go out and grab the latest tech, you need to make sure you've got all the pieces in place to make the most of it. Let's look at the first element of our equation — **Processes.**

10 / FIX YOUR PROCESSES

Perfection is achieved, not when there is nothing more to add, but when there is nothing left to take away.
–Antoine de Saint Exupery

Putting great tech on a bad process only makes that bad process faster, not better. So before you invest in tech, shore up your processes.

Refining processes shouldn't be overlooked. Remember the

story I told about Ford in the Introduction, and how they reduced headcount in A/P by 75% just by improving their processes?

Can you break a process into several repeatable steps that can be delegated downstream? The characteristics that make a task a good candidate for delegation also make it amenable to automation.

Is an estimate materially as good as the exact number? Is there a better report you can create at the beginning of your process that can eliminate a spreadsheet? Are there steps that can be eliminated without increasing risk?

Standardizing and documenting your processes reduces duplicated efforts, and in today's increasingly complex regulatory world, it helps us make sure we're not missing anything.

Once you have standard, optimized processes, it's easy to add those to a workflow tool. Putting everything in one spot also helps when you have turnover in your department, as Derek Mernagh, controller at Yelp, experiences in the highly competitive market of San Francisco:

> *It's been really helpful with FloQast, as people leave and people come in, they're able to see immediately their tasks, because we've explained every single accounting task in FloQast. So once that person joins, then they can see exactly what they need to do. And that's how to get people up to speed a lot more quickly than before. And also, it's helped the team as well to save some time where they can focus on more value-add activities.*

With optimized and standardized processes, it's a piece of cake to delegate. When Chris Sluty joined Cullen and me to co-found FloQast, he had never closed the books before. Here's what he said about that experience, which was his first job after eight years as an auditor:

It's interesting that as an auditor, you're seen as an accounting expert, but you really don't understand what people in industry do every month. I came in and the first time I ever closed the books was the FloQast books. I came in with no knowledge of the company, walked through FloQast with a month-end checklist that Mike had built out, and closed the books for the first time. I only had one or two questions for Mike, because I could see what he did in the prior period.

I was kind of the first FloQast customer. It was fascinating to me because I was essentially beta testing the software at the same time as I was learning to close the books.

DEVELOP PROCESSES

There are great cooks who can whip up something on the spot with just the ingredients they find in the cupboard. But ask them a month later to make that great pasta dish again, and they might not even remember making it. However, if it's a dish they make regularly, they probably have it down pat. But unless they write down their recipe, no one else will be able to do it.

The same principle applies for accounting processes. If they're not documented somewhere, and if that person who keeps the process in their head isn't available to do their piece of the close, the result can be chaos. It also means that no one can schedule vacations during the close. And you and your team members might miss out on the events that can't be scheduled — events like weddings, childbirth, funerals, and your kids' school and sports events.

Changing processes isn't easy, particularly if you've got team members who have been doing something the same way for years. They're not likely to change unless you can demonstrate that a new way not only saves time, but also gets a better work product.

THINK ABOUT THE WHY OF A PROCESS

All processes are paths that get you from point A to point B. They tell you What to do. But the path you've used — or that someone else figured out and taught you — isn't always the best way to get there. Understanding the Why of a process can give you a shortcut that someone else didn't know existed. Here's an example from my days at Cornerstone.

> *We were getting ready for the S1, and it was just chaos. Arguing with lawyers and drafting things up, and it was well after 5 pm. My SEC reporting manager came to me and started assigning me tasks.*
>
> *First, she gave me two lists of customers and told me to reconcile names between the two spreadsheets. I was supposed to cross out the names of customers who were on both lists. So I got that done, and she gave me another list that I had to go through line by line and match transactions. I got through that exercise after spending a couple hours on it. It was getting close to midnight, and it was just crazy. The lawyers were still there, and still working on the S1.*
>
> *Finally, I kind of snapped and asked my SEC manager, "Why am I doing this?" She told me, "I was just trying to understand what customers we have in the media."*
>
> *So I had done all this work, but if she had told me upfront why she needed me to go through this mess of a process, I could have just gone to NetSuite and run a report in about 90 seconds that would have given her the answer.*
>
> *She didn't know what I knew, so she was trying to explain to me the way she would do it as someone who had never logged into NetSuite. She was telling me What to do, instead of Why to do it.*

That experience has stuck with me. I was so frustrated with burning about four hours of my time and a couple hours of her time in walking me through What she wanted me to do. If she had just told me Why she needed me to do the work, we would have been done in less than two minutes.

TAKING THE TIME TO EXPLAIN THE WHY PAYS OFF

One of the main problems in accounting is that our deadlines are so tight, it's hard to take the time to explain to people why we should be doing something. For a manager, it's more time consuming to explain the end goal, the why of what a process is trying to achieve. It takes more conversations. Then you have to trust the person to get on board with it and get it done. Generally the person training someone else knows how to do that work, so they're just going to tell someone what to do.

The worst offender is just telling someone SALY. Go look at last year and copy that. It's not a very inspirational form of work. But in audit, it's easier to tell someone to follow last year than to sit them down and explain that the reason we audit companies is basically to prove that the financials are materially correct. And that's really important for the stakeholders who rely on those financials to make investment or other decisions. Then you walk through the audit methodology.

Going into detail with the Why of accounting is a good use of their time if you want to train your people, but it's not a good use of your time if you want to hit a deadline.

But if you're a controller, and the What you're doing is already documented, then you should have more time for specific one-off projects. For those special projects, you should have more time to sit down with your person and explain why you're doing something. If they're smart, you can trust them to figure out how they can get it done.

Here's an example from my last project at Cornerstone. The CEO and CFO sat me down for 30 minutes and told me that

Cornerstone had acquired a company out of New Zealand. It was in a different currency and using different GAAP. They were on Xero, and we were on NetSuite. My bosses told me that they didn't do much due diligence, and that they wanted the new company's operations to be completely folded into Cornerstone. They needed me to do everything required to make that happen. That was the gist of what they told me. They explained the situation to me and Why I needed to do this work.

Not to think too highly of myself, but I think I'm pretty smart and can figure stuff out. So they let me run with it for two months, and I gave them the Mike Whitmire completed audit package for the company. I told them, "I think you way overpaid for it." And I had everything ready to bring operations into the fold.

All they needed to do was sit me down for 30 minutes and explain Why I was doing this, and then let me do the work. They didn't need to tell me What to do.

IMPROVING PROCESSES IS A TEAM EFFORT

The first step in standardizing and improving your processes is to get everyone in the same room, and have an open and transparent discussion about how everyone performs specific tasks. You've got to get input from both those pushing to innovate and those who resist innovation the most.

Once everyone's ideas are on the table, then as a team, brainstorm new ways of doing the work. If you have a large and unwieldy team, you may need to work with a subset of that group or on your own to develop new ways of doing a task. Be sure at every step to include input from the naysayers.

Once you get buy-in from the people who are actually going

to do the work, you'll have a much easier time moving the change forward.

CHECKLISTS FOR THE BORING STUFF

We accountants love checklists, but every now and again, I run into a controller who says they don't need them because they've got all their processes in their heads. As Shivang Patel, Director of Sales Ops here at FloQast told me, "complacency produces errors." It's easy to skip a step, or make an assumption. And then you've got problems.

One of Cullen's favorite books is Atul Gawande's *The Checklist Manifesto.* According to Gawande, the beauty of checklists is that they take care of the routine, boring stuff:

> The checklist gets the dumb stuff out of the way, the routines your brain shouldn't have to occupy itself with, and lets it rise above to focus on the hard stuff.

As the book explains, doctors and airplane pilots benefit beyond making sure that steps aren't forgotten when they use checklists, according to Cullen:

By merely checking things off the list, they get mental clarity. Just being able to focus on the task they are presented with next instead of thinking about the totality of everything that has to get done.

That is just not the way we as humans work best.

Documenting what's in your head — and what's in the heads of everyone on your team — puts an end to tribal knowledge. According to our 2017 survey on the chaos of the month-end close,[1] 71% of finance professionals said that their teams work primarily with tribal knowledge.

This is a huge risk if that one person leaves the company or can't do the work because of a family or health emergency. What would happen if a key person were hit by the proverbial bus? What impact would that have on the financial operations of the company?

With documented processes in place, you don't need to keep all the steps in your head. You can put them in a checklist. With a checklist, you can delegate, and that frees you up to focus on the harder stuff. Or, better yet, you can automate those processes by adding in the right tools.

Having processes in place reduces your risk because you know that the way something will be done this month is the same as it was done last month, and the month before. It's consistent. You can trust your numbers. You can spend your time investigating the outliers and anomalies instead of compiling information. Your auditors will like that consistency.

DO YOUR PROCESSES AND YOUR TECH PLAY NICELY TOGETHER?

But before you put too much time into re-engineering your processes, consider how technology will integrate with them. You'll get better results with automation if you take a holistic approach and look at the entire end-to-end processes, like data-to-report, purchase-to-pay or order-to-cash instead of taking a piecemeal approach, and automating a step here and there. As researchers at McKinsey Global found when they surveyed automation initiatives around the world in 2017:[2]

> The temptation for managers as they implement an automation program is to follow that same pattern, retrofitting a particular automation tool into the existing process. Moreover, managers often see automation as a technology initiative that can be led by the IT department. As a result, companies end up with a patchwork of incongruous technology tools that automate separate and

> distinct parts of the process. This approach is fine for capturing the first five% or so of automation's impact.

Unlocking the full potential requires a fundamentally different way of thinking. To capture that potential, managers must be willing to reengineer their processes completely.

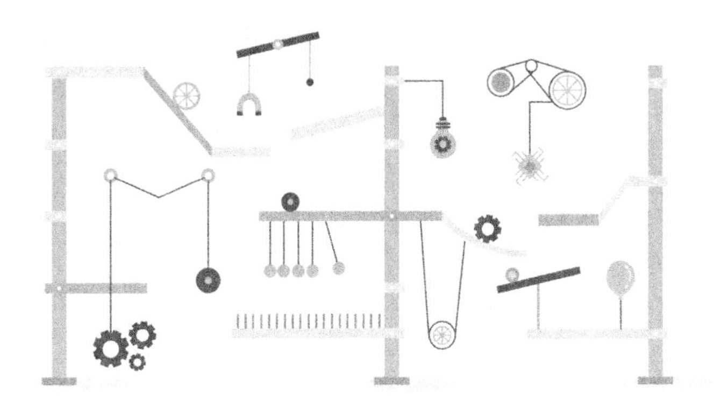

The problems that McKinsey Global found back in 2017 haven't gone away. Accountants need to be part of any tech changes that will impact them. You don't want a patchwork of tools that don't work together. You want an integrated whole that works in symphony.

Instead of trying to customize apps and software to fit your current process, consider whether adopting processes that are assumed by tech tools will give you a better solution. Many of these (but not all) follow the best-of-breed processes that many others have found to be the most effective and the most efficient.

You and your team might have to make some big changes, but if you choose your tech wisely, those changes will be for the better. They won't require workarounds to fit your work into a new process that's not flexible enough to capture the calculations that are part of what you do every month. Using bots to automate a newly designed process instead of humans can minimize the disruption, and get your team out of the muck of a tedious, error-prone manual process.

Which takes us to the next element: **Tools**. When you choose the right tools and add them to an efficient process, you can reduce chaos. Plus, you'll have more time and bandwidth to focus on reducing risk and helping to make your company as strong as possible.

11 / WHAT'S IN YOUR TOOLBOX?

Technology presumes there's just one right way to do things and there never is.
–Robert M. Pirsig

Traditionally, accounting and finance have been the parts of the company that get the last bite of the apple when it comes to technology. Some of that may be because the older mainframe ERPs cost a fortune and were tough to implement. Not to mention that accounting has traditionally been seen as a cost center, not a profit center.

Our Product Manager, Erika Hecksher, is a veteran of public accounting and finance departments in many industries, and has seen the transition from paper-based accounting through early versions of Oracle to today's cloud ERPs. Here's what she says about why so many accountants get last priority in technology:

> *Accounting is the last place that gets technology because there is very little perceived benefit. You're closing the books. If you're closing the books, why do you need technology? Are the numbers wrong?*
>
> *No, you can't say the numbers are wrong. The numbers are right.*
>
> *But then why do you need technology? Is it the cost of the accounting department?*
>
> *It's not really the cost of the accounting department, because they're all run very leanly.*
>
> *It's the failure of providing an opportunity for the accountants to actually understand what's going on with the numbers, and to make the numbers more useful for management.*
>
> *Because they don't have the time to do it. They just fundamentally don't have the time to do it. The only way you can give them the time to do it is to provide the technology that gets the work done for them.*

I saw this reluctance to invest in tech firsthand when I was doing contracts at Cornerstone. There was a software tool that would have saved us a ton of time, and would have allowed us to scale without adding much headcount. But it cost something like $30,000 a year, so they said no. If we had implemented that, then instead of having 11 people when I left, we probably would have had three or four to do that job: a system admin and a couple of people to validate the data and make sure it's going in properly, and then check the guidance and administer it.

But instead, they hired Big Four auditors to do the work that technology could have. So instead of spending $30,000 on software, they spent probably around half a million hiring eight Big Four auditors at $70,000 a pop. It was just crazy.

The goal, as Derek Mernagh, controller at Yelp, says is to put in place processes and automation so your company can grow without adding headcount.

> *As you're scaling the business, and as the business continues to grow, you have to have the infrastructure in place to make sure that you can scale without adding headcount all of the time. When you get to a point where you're growing, and you can keep up with the pace of growth without adding additional headcount, then I think you've reached the right level of systems in place and automation.*
>
> *But if you don't ensure that your team is implementing the right technology and the right tools, then they're going to just be focused on the extra manual tasks that are in place, because you're a growing company. You really have to look for opportunities and partner with the financial systems team to make sure that you're automating as much as possible. And when you have the ability to automate and cut manual tasks, then you actually give your team the opportunity to focus on more value-add tasks.*
>
> *And that's so important. You know, you don't want to be at a place where you have all of these nice-to-do's and things that you should be doing. But you can't because you're constantly working on manual tasks to close the books.*

The status quo for a long time has been to throw more human bodies at the work instead of investing in tech. Fortunately, as younger people like me and Derek Mernagh start rising through the ranks, modern controllers want more from their jobs than to be compiling and reporting data. They see tech as crucial for helping with strategy, as my co-founder Chris says:

> *Accounting has been a cost center, ultimately. But the hope is for the modern controller to use accounting to be more strategic. Strategy has typically fallen on the shoulders of the CFO. The CFO needs to trust what accounting's doing, and has to have good faith in the numbers in order to make those types of decisions.*
>
> *So the more accounting can be viewed as a strategic part of your organization and not just a cost center, the more that you flip that perception, the more will be invested in tech in that department.*

Cloud technology is changing that perception. With numbers almost in real time, for the first time, CEOs can make decisions based on real data, not merely the intuition and gut feeling that has been the best they had for the last couple of centuries.

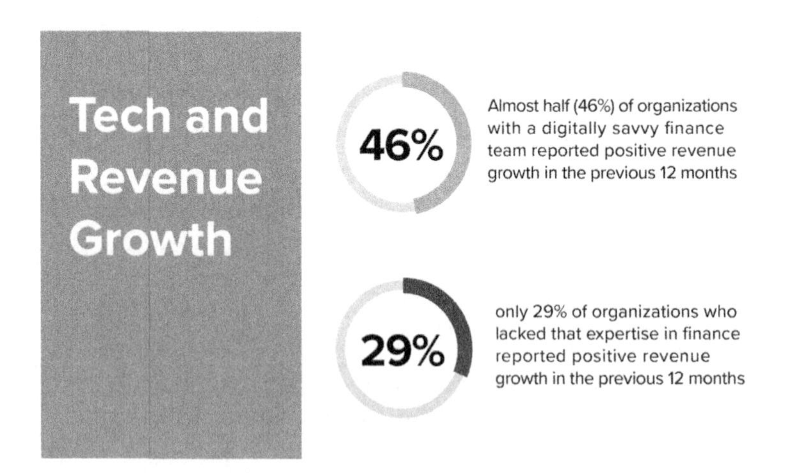

Plus the more successful a company is, the more likely it is to have invested in technology for the finance team, according to an AICPA / CIMA report.[1] Almost half (46%) of organizations with a digitally savvy finance team reported positive revenue growth in the previous 12 months, compared to only 29% of organizations who lacked that expertise in finance.

Now I concede that this is just another correlation, not causation, but if Kurzweil is right, and we're in the second half of the chessboard of technology transformation, you don't want to be climbing a Mt. Everest of technology just to catch up.

The good news is there are many more robust options out there, and more finance executives report that they plan on implementing tech in the coming year. A 2019 survey by Grant Thornton of nearly 400 senior finance executives[2] found that a good chunk of respondents intend to increase their use of emerging technologies for accounts payable and accounts receivable (46%), financial reporting and control (44%), financial planning and analysis (43%), tax and compliance (43%), budgeting and forecasting (42%), and corporate development and strategy (41%).

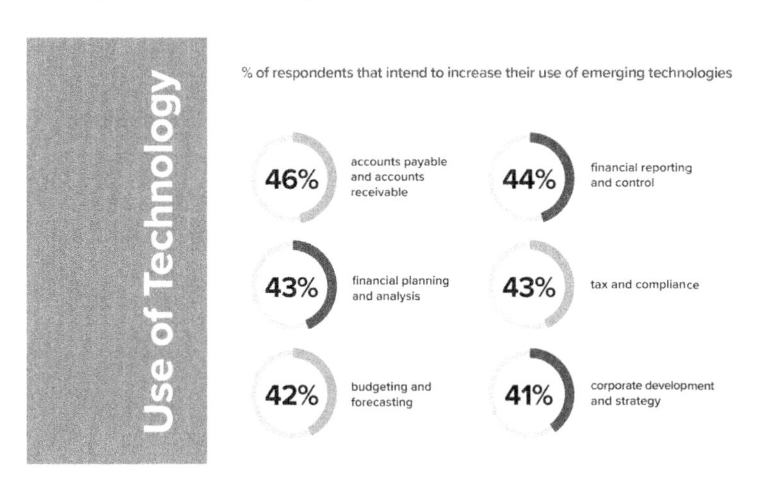

The ROI on these new tech investments won't be measured just by cutting costs and making processes more efficient. As Grant Thornton's survey notes, finance leaders will now need to "approach technology investments through the value lens, finding ways to increase the value of intangibles like customer satisfaction."

Adding more tech also means that accountants will finally be free of the mind-numbing manual work we've done for generations, and we'll be able to truly contribute to our organizations in ways beyond building those perfect spreadsheet masterpieces.

Accounting will become the coolest job at the company.

So here are some questions to think about as you consider new technology:

- How will this technology benefit us in the long run?
- Do we already have other tools to do this?
- Do we need this?
- Where do we see this tech developing?
- What does the future for the company that makes this tool look like?
- Will they be around long enough and will they keep innovating?
- What do others say about using this tech and working with their customer success team?
- What tools are my competitors using?
- How will this enhance the experience of our customers?

Review Note: Reduce the risks of Excel

Excel is the favorite tool of accountants worldwide. It can do almost anything we need to do in our jobs. It's easy to use, easy to share, and by mastering just a few functions and macros, we can pull amazing insights out of a mass of raw data.

But as articles in the Wall Street Journal[3] and Forbes[4] point out, Excel has problems. Because it's so easy to send by email, there might be a dozen or so versions of the same spreadsheet flying around. Which one is right? Are any of them correct or complete? There's no audit trail, so it's impossible to tell who made changes or when. And unless you lock it down, anyone can make changes later. Rolling spreadsheets forward can also be problematic if it's done manually.

All of these problems mean that if you're using Excel for complex accounting, such as tracking your leases or revenue recognition, you'll never be SOX 404 compliant.

Some people think these issues mean that it's past time for Excel to be gone. But so far, the alternatives such as web forms are seriously lacking the flexibility and functionality of Excel. They're clunky and hard to use. They don't work the way we work. They don't have the formulas we need. Many accountants still use Excel to get numbers to feed into those web forms.

Here's what Greg Vecellio, our controller at FloQast, told me about closing the books at his previous company, a global company with multiple consolidations, an Excel-heavy exercise:

> *We had to certify that everything was done, and then I'd go in the next month and it wouldn't be in balance. And then you'd have to start the whole process of trying to figure out what happened. And it was a month ago, so nobody remembers. You don't catch it until the following month. So, there was a whole lack of visibility. And the inability to really feel like you were in control of your close. And then I felt like the close controlled me more than I controlled the close. Because you just never knew, and you could just never relax to say, yeah, I know we're good, I know nothing's changing. We're in a good spot.*

Here at FloQast, we have a different solution. Instead of

completely ditching Excel, we say you should mitigate those risks by layering a close management system on top that locks down prior periods, automates the roll forward and leaves an audit trail.

This lets you keep working the way you've always worked, but with less risk.

REDUCE YOUR INADVERTENT ADHD TENDENCIES

Being a controller can be worse than herding cats. You've got pressure on you to get the work done quickly, and a lot of moving pieces that all need to come together before you can get on to the next big part of your work. Even though we know that multitasking isn't how to improve efficiency and effectiveness in our work, we have so many things going on that we are forced to switch between tasks just so we can keep things moving.

But tech tools can help us regain our lives, by "removing at least some of the chaos," as Cullen Zandstra says.

> *We as humans are just not built to multitask. And I think that a lot of times accountants are forced to think about a lot of different stuff, all at the same time, especially during the close. What our product really aims to do is remove at least some of those things that you have to multitask.*
>
> *If you can say for sure that the reconciliations all tie up, then that is one thing that I know I don't have to think about. I don't have to think about it until the system alerts me that I need to think about it. I'm not distracted by some other problem that I don't want to worry about. So I'm able to refocus on the things that humans are really good at.*
>
> *Humans are just not that great at keeping track of things and remembering things verbatim. That's just not how our brains work.*

Tech tools that help us remember tasks and alert us when a human needs to take a look at something buy us the mental bandwidth and time to focus on what we do best.

WHAT TECHNOLOGY DO I NEED TO KNOW ABOUT?

It's virtually impossible to learn everything about all the new technologies, while keeping up with the latest FASB pronouncements, plus knowing what's going on in your industry, and what's happening inside your company. But you should have at least a passing knowledge of the tech that's out there. And it's a good idea to reach out to the IT department to make sure everyone is on the same page for appropriate technology for your organization.

Here are some technologies that have promise for finance:

Automation and robotics: Repetitive, no-brainer type activities are prime for automation. Letting tech do the boring work gives you and your team more time and bandwidth to do more interesting strategic work. A recent report by McKinsey Global,[5] *Harnessing Automation for a Future that Works,* has examples of the kinds of accounting tasks that can be automated.

Data visualization: Outside of finance, most people in our organizations don't understand the language of numbers. But if we can put that data in a graph, a pie chart, or an animation, we can communicate the ideas behind the numbers to stakeholders or to others in our organization. Check out the endnotes for a link to a page by Tableau,[6] which features data visualizations throughout history, from Napoleon's ill-fated march to Moscow to changes in the age of the U.S. population in time.

Artificial intelligence and machine learning: While there has been fear-mongering in recent years that AI will take away our jobs, a more realistic view is that AI will augment our work and help us with the talent crunch. Robust applications to process A/R, A/P, and expense reports using AI have already alleviated the tedium of data entry. For example, here at FloQast, we're using AI in our AutoRec product to automate account reconciliations.

Blockchain: Some say this will completely change the way accounting is done, and may put auditors out of business. Others say this is hype and that blockchain isn't yet ready for prime time, if it ever will be. But according to a 2019 report by Grant Thornton,[7] 22% of finance executives surveyed have already implemented blockchain, and another 24% plan to implement it in the next 12 months. These finance executives were from firms with revenues between $100 million and $20 billion, so it may take deep pockets to implement blockchain.

HOW DO TECH TOOLS REDUCE RISK?

The most obvious way tech tools reduce risk is by reducing the errors that come from manual data entry or inconsistent application of processes. Even the most adept ten-key user occasionally fat-fingers a number or two, but automation eliminates those kinds of errors.

Leveraging technology also helps us create time and capacity to think about our work. By automating the assembly, reporting, and some of the basic analysis of finance, technology creates the bandwidth needed to support your organization. With so much of recent FASB updates relying on estimates, controllers need time to review the calculations and assumptions used to generate those estimates. Errors in these estimates can be material, so it's essential that we get the inputs right.

A recent article in the New York Times reminds us that implementing technology can also prevent the kinds of fraud that allowed one Long Island Railroad maintenance worker to record 72 hours of overtime on top of his regular 40 hours per week.[8] Even though the railroad had installed biometric time clocks which required employees to use their thumbprint to scan in and out of work, union employees had a special dispensation which allowed them to use paper timesheets, which apparently were simply rubber-stamped with no scrutiny or consideration of their reasonableness.

Biometric security like the Long Island Railroad had in place — but didn't implement — will be one of the tools we'll see more of in the future. When you combine tech tools with efficient and effective processes, you lay the foundation for the next piece of our equation: **Knowledge**.

12 / KNOWLEDGE CONNECTS EVERYTHING

Knowledge is power. Information is power. The secreting or hoarding of knowledge or information may be an act of tyranny camouflaged as humility.
–Robin Morgan

Now that you see how processes and tools work together, you're ready to start on the knowledge piece. As I said earlier, grafting the latest tech onto bad or outdated processes might save you some time, but it won't help you much with overcoming the barriers to risk management that arise from the inability to understand and analyze your data.

Better processes will save you time, effort, and will get you more accurate information. Adding tools to automate those processes buys you the mental space you need to step back and think about your work. Then layering on applications for analytics and data visualization will help you look at your numbers in a new light.

KNOW WHEN TO PUSH BACK ON THE AUDITORS

When the auditor says you have to do something differently, the traditional controller would acquiesce and just do it. Because I have a better understanding and intrinsic knowledge of the different parts of my company, I look at their requests from the point of view of what's best for the company rather than what might make the auditors happy.

Recently, our auditors were pushing accounting to get significantly more information from engineering to get calculations for a capitalized software account. Filling out that spreadsheet that the auditors wanted would have taken a huge amount of their time, and we would have lost a ton of productivity.

It's my job to protect the accounting department, but it's also my job to do what's in the best interest of the company. Five years ago when I was an accountant, I would never have thought about pushing back on a request from the auditors. I would have gone to engineering and said that we need this report every month to pass the audit. I would not have cared about the overall impact it would have on the business when engineers have to fill out spreadsheets when they should be coding instead.

Instead, since I have a broader understanding of the business, I went to the auditors and I said, "There's no way I'm doing this. It's way too burdensome on my engineering team. That's the team that produces product which builds our business." I respect them as auditors, but I said it just couldn't be that way. We could either have no capitalized software account, or we could get to a reasonable compromise. So we ended up getting to a compromise, where the number is going to be materially correct every month, but the onus to make sure it's materially correct is placed on the auditors, and I've taken the vast majority of the work off my team's plate.

By pushing back like that, I'm willing to take the risk that the capitalized software account might be off by 10% in a given month. But the reality is, in the stage of business development we're at, and with the stakeholders we have to communicate with, no one but the auditors will care if that account bounces around month to month.

Let's say that instead, I agreed to what the auditors requested. Now I'll have my whole team submit their hours and the managers will approve it. Then the VP will look at it. Then we'll analyze the projects and we'll decide that 73.4% of our hours should be capitalized last month. And let's say we do that every month.

On the one hand, we're going to pass the audit with flying colors. There's going to be no risk there. It's going to be great and the four people in the audit room are all going to be really happy.

On the other hand, what might happen is our product rollouts are going to slow down. We might not go to market as quickly as we planned. Our entire business and fundraising is based on the timing of delivery of those products. So now, we're adding business risk that could result in the company going out of business. I would much rather fail an audit than go out of business.

The decision I made might not be the right decision for every company. But as a modern controller, you've got to take a business-minded approach, and look at the holistic view of what's best for the company, and not just roll over when the auditor tells you to do something.

REDUCE RISK BY EMBRACING RISK

It sounds crazy, but to reduce risk, you need to embrace risk. One of the keys to embracing risk in a safe way is to change your focus from GAAP and the rear-view mirror of the past to the big windshield of the present and the future.

I'm not saying controllers should be irresponsible with your organization's resources or that they should skate close to the line of ethics, but to thrive in the new world, organizations need to be willing to try new things, to experiment, and to be willing to fail sometimes. Being a strategic partner for your organization means you need to lean in and embrace risk.

As I mentioned above, we're in a period of accelerating technological change. Companies that lag behind in implementing tech tend also to be overall risk-averse, as a joint study between Deloitte and MIT Sloan Management found.[1] In 2016, they surveyed 3,500 managers and executives from 117 countries, and divided the respondents' organizations into three groups according to their degree of digital implementation and digital transformation: early-stage, developing, and maturing. Only 29% of respondents from early-stage companies said their organizations accepted risk as part of experimenting with new initiatives, in contrast to 71% of maturing companies.

Digitally maturing companies demonstrated a distinct culture from early-stage companies. Respondents from maturing companies were much more likely to agree with these statements:

- Their companies were working to increase agility.
- Experimentation and testing were encouraged as a form of learning.
- Their companies encouraged collaboration.
- Their workforces tended to be organized in cross-functional teams.

One of the best ways to avoid unnecessary risk is simply to be aware of as many possible risks as you can be. Today's modern controllers can't stay in the silo of accounting and just pay attention to the numbers and whether the GL ties to the reconciliations.

INCREASE YOUR KNOWLEDGE TO REDUCE RISK

The first step is to learn everything you can about your organization and its place in the marketplace. You need to be aware of what the competition is doing. You need to also be looking ahead and anticipating what the future will bring.

What are the concerns of the other departments in your organization? What keeps the members of the C-suite and upper management up at night? These are some of the questions that can help answer the **Why** we do the work piece of our equation:

Technology = Process + Tools + Knowledge

You may also need to get others in your organization on board with making sure they're diligent about providing the information needed for complete and accurate analysis. As an article at IT Pro Portal points out,[2] this may mean educating your sales teams about the importance of fully and consistently updating CRM tools, which aren't always the most user-friendly. As the author says, updating the information in a CRM is "perceived by the majority of those working within a business as an administrative task rather than of strategic value; essentially a great big spreadsheet that captures data for management or operations teams only."

By demonstrating how this information plays a crucial role across the organization, and how complete, accurate, and up-to-date information can help those entering the data do their jobs better, you'll increase the odds that they'll be more diligent.

One of the really cool things about today compared to the world that the older generations grew up in is the amount of information we have at our fingertips. At Cornerstone, when I was assigned that project to fold an acquired company into our operations, and had to convert New Zealand GAAP into US GAAP, I learned a lot of what I needed to know on Google. I didn't have to sit down with a Big Four partner or another technical person to figure that out. I could just look that up on my own.

Having the access to all that information allows people who want to learn to self-educate. If they're motivated, they can take that knowledge and grow their own careers. They don't have to depend on someone above them dishing out advice or guidance. They can learn beyond what's expected for their role and they can use that knowledge to move far beyond their traditional role.

In the future, agility will become more important. Agility isn't just being able to turn on a dime, and rapidly change directions when the marketplace changes (although that's important, too). It's also about understanding how you can help your organization better serve all its stakeholders.

As Jim Bell, former CFO and current CEO of PF Chang's said in an article on CFO.com:

> I think of agility as the constant, timely transfer of business acumen to financial performance. Seen from that lens, agility quickly becomes not just a nice-to-have, but a strategic imperative.[3]

As Bell points out in that article, bringing automation to the planning process made it possible for his finance team at PF Chang's to dig into issues as they came up, and to disseminate knowledge about the company's performance to the people who needed that information to make strategic decisions.

I agree that leaning into risk might feel uncomfortable. We accountants are known for being risk-averse. That may account for why some accounting teams are slow to implement new technologies: we don't want to invest in something that's not proven and have it fail on us. And as custodians and guardians of the resources of our organizations, we're reluctant to invest in things that don't end up working.

We're not used to experimenting, and we certainly don't want to fail. In the rest of our work, anything less than 100% accuracy is unacceptable. But to keep up with the exponential rate of change in technology, we need to embrace a culture of experimentation.

Remember what Shivang said about chasing gold medals or running away from German Shepherds? This is a good way to think about taking risks. Most people make big changes when the pain of not changing exceeds the pleasure of not making the effort to change, when that German Shepherd is nipping at their heels. But another motivation for change is the reward of that gold medal when we put in the extra effort.

The German Shepherds here are the pain of doing things the way we've always done them. The manual processes, the error-prone spreadsheets, and the fear that our competition will leave us in the dust.

The gold medal is the promise of a new future where processes are automated, and where technology gives us the mental capacity to think about our work, and to do more of the fun stuff.

Review Note: Reduce the risk of losing your talent

As I mentioned in the last section, our survey[4] of controllers found that 88% had been approached for a new career opportunity outside their current job in the previous 12 months. Well over half of controllers (59%) reported that they would consider leaving their current job if the right opportunity came to them.

Don't forget that study by Harvard Business Review[5] I mentioned earlier that found that organizations with outdated office tech were having a hard time keeping the best people onboard. That study also found that job candidates were factoring in the state of a company's technology when deciding which job offer to accept.

It's not just the technology at a company that impacts retention — it's also the commitment of organizations to developing digital skills in their teams, as Deloitte and MIT Sloan Research found in their 2016 survey.[6] At companies that did not provide opportunities to improve digital skills, VP-level leaders were 15 times as likely to say they planned to leave that company in a year than companies who provided learning and development opportunities.

With a shortage of talent, it's vital that our organizations step up their efforts in improving the skills of everyone, especially in digital technologies. What got us our jobs won't get us to the future. Lifetime learning is an imperative for everyone.

MCW

DO YOU KNOW THE RIGHT THINGS ABOUT YOUR ORGANIZATION?

There's a Peter Drucker quote that gets passed around as gospel truth:

"What gets measured gets managed."

The idea behind this quote is that unless you can measure something, you can't manage it. The problem is that sometimes the easiest things to quantify — like costs or profit — aren't always the best things to measure. Obsessing too much about the bottom line can actually do more harm than good.

The good news is that according to some people who have read a lot more of Peter Drucker's books than I have, he never said that. What he did say about knowledge workers in *The*

Effective Executive is that "Working on the right things is what makes knowledge work effective."

So how do we as accountants and knowledge workers know what those right things are? One thing is for sure — it's not GAAP measurements. If you spend too much time deep in the weeds, and GAAP numbers are the only numbers you pay attention to, that won't be much help for the CFO or the others above you. The CFO doesn't need to know anything about EBITDA.

The reality is that external people don't care about GAAP information. They care about the metrics that are specific to that industry. So for me, working in the SaaS world, I need to know my SaaS metrics inside and out, like none other. No one cares about EBITDA, but you better know your LTV to CAC ratio. Those are forward-looking ratios.

I hate saying that as an accountant, but that is the reality. When our auditors forced us to capitalize software, our VC investors wanted to know why we were doing that. That account just raised more questions with our stakeholders.

GAAP is the rear view mirror, and it's what I focused on in my years at EY. What helped me make that transition from backward-looking to forward-looking was really understanding in detail the non-GAAP metrics that a SaaS company focuses on.

The metrics we care about are things that help us grow going forward. The metrics that matter reflect whether or not we're making our customers happy.

The reality is that the vast majority of the money in the stock market is institutional dollars and investments from hedge funds. Their investment decisions are definitely based on quarterly results, but when they decide to take big positions in companies, that's really driven by future opportunities.

They're not investing in the company as it is today, but what that company is going to be in five years.

It's disturbing to me that GAAP financials aren't viewed as having a ton of value because they're not necessarily aligned with the business. That's consistent with what Baruch Lev and Feng Gu found when they did an exhaustive analysis of the importance of financial reports on stock prices which they describe in their book, *The End of Accounting.*

Lev and Gu point out that even though businesses have changed dramatically over the past century from heavy asset-based manufacturing to information intensive intangibles-based tech companies, the general format of financial reporting has hardly changed at all. A balance sheet from 1912 looks a whole lot like one from 2019.

According to their analysis, back in the 50s, about 90% of the stock price could be attributed to a company's earnings as reported in their financials.[7] But today, only about 5% of the stock price comes from information in a company's financial reports.[8] The rest comes from SEC filings, analysts' reports, and what Lev and Gu call "non-transactional business events," which include things like success or failure of drugs or software, strategic moves by the company, contracts signed or canceled, and new regulations.[9]

This means that as a controller, you need to learn everything you can about your organization and the plans for the future. You can't stay in the weeds of GAAP, looking backwards. You need to change your focus to the future, and how metrics today impact that future.

Review Note: Are you measuring the right things about your company?

The concept of key metrics isn't new, by the way. As Ronald Baker details in his 2006 book, *Measure What Matters to Customers: Using Key Predictive Indicators*[10], Gordon Bethune steered Continental Airlines from worst airline to best airline in the mid-1990s by paying attention to the three metrics that customers care about:

- Lost luggage
- On-time arrival
- Customer complaints

One thing to notice about those metrics is that they're not financial. They're not available from Continental's accounting system. And they're things that most everyone working at Continental could impact positively.

These metrics are also more about the Why of Continental than the What of Continental. The What for Continental was to survive as a going concern. The Why was creating an airline that people wanted to fly on. And by focusing on these non-financial metrics, Continental's finances improved.

If you don't know where your organization is trying to go, you can't be of any help in achieving that goal.

MCW

WHAT ARE THE MOST IMPORTANT THINGS FOR YOUR CUSTOMERS?

I'm pretty sure your customers don't buy your products or services because your results last quarter exceeded the analysts' predictions. Do they save money or time with your solution? Or is your customer service legendary? What about time-to-value for your customers? Or does your company have a powerful social mission that appeals to your ideal customers? Are they loyal because they resonate with your Why?

By focusing on the things that your customers most value, and working to improve those, you reduce risk. As I said earlier, you've got to also have one eye on future trends. You've got to be anticipating what your customers will want in the future.

All this talk about what customers want is definitely way outside what the traditional controller does. But I'm mentioning this here because to be the modern controller, you need to be more of a strategic partner to the rest of your organization.

And remember, your customers aren't just the people who buy the products and services your organization makes. You have internal customers who need your help in understanding how their efforts impact the company as a whole.

Are there metrics that would be helpful to them? Those three metrics that Gordon Bethune monitored are **leading indicators**. Changes in leading indicators give you an idea of where the company is headed. They're like the canaries that coal miners used to carry with them as an early warning system for toxic levels of carbon monoxide. They correlate with something that will happen in the future.

So for sales, a leading indicator might be "number of demos requested." Or maybe "number of unique visitors" on a sales page. What about levels of use by customers? Changes in regular patterns of usage can indicate there's a problem, and a quick check-in call might help keep them on board.

As accountants, we have our finger on the pulse of the financial performance of our organizations. But we have to figure out how to combine the numbers we have with the non-financial data so we can help the folks in marketing, in sales, in operations, and in all the other parts of the organization. This is where data visualization in the form of do-it-yourself dashboards will make you a hero.

THINK CUSTOMER FIRST

Happy employees ensure happy customers. And happy customers ensure happy shareholders—in that order.
–Simon Sinek

What is it like for customers to interact with your organization? Customer experience, or CX for short, is a hot topic in marketing these days, and for good reason. A great CX makes your company's offering seem more valuable — and thus worthy of a higher price and less churn — than the competition, especially if they have a pretty sucky interface.

Think of the differences between an upscale luxury resort and the Motel 6. Both give you essentially the same thing: a private room with a bed and a bathroom. But the moment you walk in the lobby and start interacting with the front desk staff, your expectations are set. That's why you're probably willing to fork over five to ten times as much for a room at the Ritz than at the local budget hotel.

Now take a look at the ways your company interacts with customers and prospects. As a controller, you might not have much say in the matter, but this crucial area is something that you might be called on to measure. This will require a different approach to determine the ROI of technology investments in intangibles such as customer satisfaction rather than simply looking at increases in sales revenue.

Are there ways that your organization can use technology to enhance the customer experience? Don't limit your consideration to the outward-facing aspects of your organization like customer support, but consider the ways that your customers interact with back office functions.

Are there ways to redesign the process that would make it

easier for customers to make payments, query their order status, or check on service requests? Many of these improvements also have the benefit of making it easier for the accounting team to do their jobs.

For SaaS companies, taking a customer-first approach is part of the business model. At FloQast, I like to say that we emphasize the Service just as much as the Software. Our customers aren't just one-off buyers. It's not just a business transaction. They become an integral part of our company.

This is a mindset shift. To keep our customers happy, we have to pay attention to their needs and how they interact with the software. We have to anticipate what features will delight them before they ask for those features. We make the implementation process as easy and as fast as possible. When a customer has an issue, we need to take care of it right away.

According to the AICPA/CIMA report, *Agile Finance Unleashed,* "Companies that have not embraced this digital, customer-first way of working are struggling to stay relevant in their industries and with their customers."[11] In today's social media world, you can count on unexpectedly poor customer service being immediately broadcast throughout the internet.

Now, keep in mind that the external customers of your organization aren't the only customers you serve. As custodians of your organization's data, the accounting department is in a position to help more than just the C-suite.

What if you think of the rest of your organization as **your customers**?

Are there ways that you can help marketing or sales or operations? Instead of being the ones who say, "No, we can't do that. It's not in the budget," what if you start looking for ways that you can really help the other areas of your company?

You may need to be proactive and let people in other departments know how you can help them with financial analysis or profitability testing. According to the Deloitte IMA survey, *Stepping Outside the Box: Elevating the Role of the Controller*, the problem may be perception if you're not getting many requests for analysis from other parts of the organization.[12] They found that controllers who fit the traditional persona received fewer requests for analysis in the areas of financial analysis, operations, cost analysis, product and customer profitability, risk analysis, and social and environmental responsibility, than the controllers who fit the strategic or mixed personas.

If other parts of your organization aren't asking you for help in these areas, this might be an indication of a gap in skills that you need to address, or it might be a perception you need to correct. As the authors of the survey noted:

> This type of problem could present a more substantial issue if more controllers are unable to align their skill sets with a company's core vision and priorities. If the perception is a controller is out of alignment with an organization's goals, or that the C-suite has the wrong perception about a controller's capabilities, a breakdown in meeting priorities and accomplishing goals can occur.

In other words, if you want to be the strategic modern controller that all of today's organizations desperately need, you might need to market yourself and your skills to the rest of the organization. You may need to let your organization know that you're not just a bean counter, you're also a business consultant.

For more ideas, see the discussion on Net Promoter Score in Chapter 2.

REPORTING WILL CHANGE IN THE FUTURE

A big promise of automation and cloud technology is the ability to increase both the accuracy and timeliness of information to the decision makers in your organization. The C-suite and upper level management will be able to make decisions based on real data, not just on their gut instinct. Better information across your organization can only reduce risk.

Technology also means that you won't be stuck cranking out report after report for internal use. Many of those reports never get read anyways. Self-service dashboards and interactive data visualization tools mean that others in your organization can access the numbers and the insights they need when they need them, and the numbers will be up to date.

We're moving into a new era, where the month-end close becomes nearly superfluous because the numbers are up to date all the time. When rote and repeatable processes are automated end-to-end, then accountants can focus their time on the exceptions and outliers, and on the areas that require judgement and estimation. An era where the controller can walk into a meeting at any time with numbers that are up to date.

That's not the reality we're in quite yet. A survey by Deloitte of 600 global finance leaders[13] found that finance teams spend 48% of their time creating and updating reports, and only 18% of their time interacting and communicating with the business. But where they have to spend time today is not where they want to spend their time. Those finance leaders said that ideally, they'd like to reverse those figures, and spend less time on reporting and more time interacting with others in the business. Some finance teams are getting there: one of the respondents said they replaced 1,000 unique reports with 50 dashboards.

Think of the bandwidth you'd have if your team replaced custom reports with dashboards. And think of the time and mental energy you'd have to think about the future and what you can do now to reduce risks in the future. As the Deloitte survey said, "The laborious grind of management and financial reporting today likely won't exist in the future. People will be insight generators, not report builders."[14]

WHAT'S REPORTED WILL CHANGE TOO

Even though the lives of controllers revolve around reporting the results of their organizations, there's a growing body of evidence that investors don't depend solely on the financial results of organizations. According to Baruch Lev and Feng Gu's research in *The End of Accounting*, which I referred to above, as much as 95% of the value of publicly traded stocks comes from information sources that are not part of their published financials.[15] A large part of that value comes from the intangible values of their proprietary knowledge, technological advantages, or other drivers of value. For pharmaceutical companies, this might be the products in the pipeline. A telecom company might be valued more on their market penetration.

When Lev began studying these intangibles he says, "It quickly became clear to me — particularly for industries such as cellular phone companies and biotechnology — that financial reports were not only completely useless, but they were and still are actually misleading."

Lev and Gu propose a new reporting framework to supplement the information in financials that will give investors the information they need. Support for the importance of this information came from an exhaustive analysis of questions raised in earnings conference calls. Their new framework focuses on "the enterprise's strategic assets; their creation, preservation, and deployment to create corporate value."[16] This reporting framework includes numeric reporting on amounts spent on research and development, acquiring customers, customer churn, as well as on workforce development and employee turnover. It also includes narratives that describe what the company is doing to identify and mitigate risks of resource infringement and disruption.

It's an interesting idea, and would probably go a long ways towards making accounting great again. But I haven't heard of anyone voluntarily implementing it, which is how Lev and Gu hope it spreads since they're not in favor of adding yet more regulatory reporting requirements on top of what we already have to do.

For SaaS companies, GAAP metrics are nearly meaningless, as Tien Tzuo points out in his book *Subscribed: Why the Subscription Model Will Be Your Company's Future — and What to Do About It.* The income statement that's been around for 500 years, since the days of Luca Pacioli, doesn't work for subscription companies for three reasons, according to Tzuo:[17]

- Traditional income statements don't differentiate between recurring and non-recurring revenue.
- Sales and marketing expenses are matched to past goods sold instead of driving future growth.
- GAAP financials are "a backward-looking picture — it's all about money already earned, expenses already paid, actions already taken."

Tzuo proposes instead a Subscription Economy income statement that focuses on annual recurring revenue:

INCOME STATEMENT

For Year Ending December 31, 2019

Beginning ARR	100
Churn	(10)
Net ARR	**90**
RECURRING COSTS:	
Cost of Goods Sold	(20)
General & Administrative	(10)
Research & Development	(20)
Recurring Profit	**40**
SALES & MARKETING	(30)
Net Operating Income	**10**
New ARR	30
Ending ARR	**120**

The focus in Tzuo's model is on ARR, which is "known recurring revenue that you can bank on." Tzuo has shared this model with other subscription companies and with analysts who cover subscription businesses. It's definitely not GAAP, but being familiar with this and other reporting models, including the one proposed by Lev and Gu, gives you different tools that help you explain the knowledge behind the numbers to others in your organization.

Besides trying out different reporting models, many organizations are including non-financial data in their reporting, according to a survey of CFOs by Grant Thornton.[18] Because we're the numbers people, our organizations look to us to keep track of, analyze, and make sense of other types of data, which includes sustainability, diversity, environmental, social, and governance. In their survey of 378 senior finance executives from companies with revenues between $100 million and over $20 billion, Grant Thornton found that reporting of nonfinancial data had increased in 2019 compared to 2018. More than a third of finance leaders reported they were devoting more resources to non-financial reporting.

When everyone has access to tech and real time data, the advantage will go to those who can make better use of it. In a CFO.com webcast, John Granato, CFO of Tradesmen International, said that using the data better will come down to "judgment, knowledge, strategy, and approach."[19] He added that success in the future will be about "utilizing the right data, not just having a lot of it. The key will be having the right management team that can decide what data is useful and act on the key outputs."

KEEPING EVERYONE ON THE SAME PAGE

Addressing all these risks requires increased collaboration and communication between all parts of your organization. So perhaps not surprisingly, one of the characteristics of digitally maturing companies identified in the Deloitte MIT Sloan Research study was their recognition of collaboration across teams and divisions as a part of the organization's culture and operating model.[20] More than 70% of the digitally maturing organizations used cross-functional teams, compared to less than 30% of early-stage organizations.

But the path to more collaboration isn't more meetings, especially when the only achievable purpose of a meeting seems to be to schedule the next meeting. Collaboration works best when everyone has a view into what everyone else is working on. That's why we included a dashboard in FloQast that lets everyone see what tasks have been assigned to whom, and who has completed those tasks. Other tools like Asana and Slack help keep everyone on the same page.

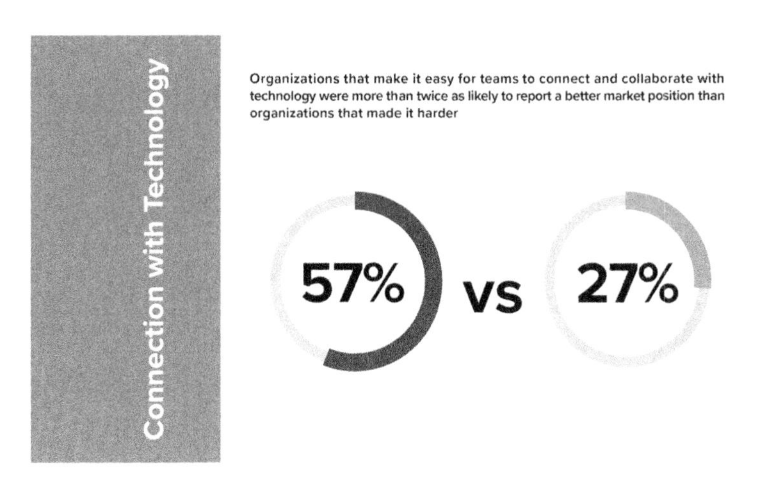

Collaboration and connectedness aren't just nice things that make your teams happier — this also makes good business sense, according to a survey by Harvard Business Review.[21] Organizations that make it easy for teams to connect and collaborate with technology were more than twice as likely to report a better market position than organizations that made it harder (57% vs. 27%). Highly-connected organizations were also more likely to report that their revenues had increased by at least 10% over the previous two years.

WHAT HAPPENS IF WE KEEP DOING WHAT WE'VE ALWAYS DONE?

The short answer is that your company may not survive the coming digital transformation. And that's the biggest risk of all. The combination of the hard trend of increased digitization and the soft trend of customer expectations of a smooth online experience means that if your organization isn't committed to doing business online, you might go the way of Blockbuster and Blackberry. Your competitors aren't likely to wait quietly on the sidelines for you to catch up.

Even if you do hang on, you'll likely have a tough time attracting and retaining talent. The trend is towards more remote and flexible work with a highly connected tech environment. Plus, you've got to be willing to invest in improving everyone's digital skills, as the Deloitte MIT study showed.[22] They found that providing opportunities for digital learning led to a 15-fold decrease in the likelihood that VP-level talent was planning on leaving in the next year.

As an added bonus, implementing tech like do-it-yourself dashboards not only gets the information in the hands of the people who need it, when they need it, but it also helps your team exit the endless cycle of creating reports because it's always been done that way.

THE OPPORTUNITY TO POSITIVELY IMPACT EVERY PART OF YOUR BUSINESS

Only a few functions in business touch every part of the organization: finance, HR, and IT. But only the finance function can translate what's happening in every part of your business into numbers, and from the numbers, create a narrative that explains what happened in the past, how the past events are impacting the present, and what that means for the future. We have the opportunity to be more than number-crunchers and report-preparers. We have the opportunity to play a strategic role in our organizations to guide them into the future. We don't have to just be the providers of information. We have the knowledge to play a major role in executing change.

PART 4
ANTICIPATING THE FUTURE

13 / CREATING THE ACCOUNTING TEAM OF THE FUTURE

The only thing we know about the future is that it will be different.
–Peter Drucker

Who could have predicted the smartphone back in 2000? And who could have predicted that today, instead of desktop and mainframe software, we'd be using apps on smartphones, and working anywhere, anytime, from almost any device?

What that tells us is that the future will be different from the present in ways that we can't yet imagine. We also know that technology will continue to play a big role in our lives, and that we'll likely see tech breakthroughs just as dramatic and life-changing as the internet, the PC, cloud accounting, and the smartphone within the decade.

In *The Future of the Professions,* Richard and Daniel Susskind said, "The least likely future for technology is that our systems will stay as they are today."[1]

Getting to that future will take effort, and will mean embracing innovation. As FloQast Product Manager Erika Heckscher told me:

> *If you want change, you have to create an environment for your staff that allows them to change and encourages them to find better ways of doing things.*
>
> *It's very hard to get accountants to change. Very often the reason that they don't change is because management doesn't want to change because when there are mistakes, it's usually because of a change. So there's a huge resistance to change. But I think the drawback is that they're going to lose staff because staff are going to leave. The ones who can improve your business are going to go somewhere where change is possible.*

Let's revisit our main formula and see what we can predict about the future, and how that will impact controllers in the future.

Success = Culture + Technology

SUCCESS

How we define success in the future may change as well. As more companies are beginning to report on sustainability, diversity, social, and environmental results, and not just on the bottom line, I predict that success for companies will be measured increasingly in non-financial terms. After all, if Baruch Lev is correct,[2] only 5% of the price of stocks is related directly to the financials.

Even the SEC is looking at the ways that the emphasis on quarterly performance is impacting long-term investors, and is considering ways to reduce the reporting burden for public companies.[3] And a recent story in the Wall Street Journal[4] reports that the business leaders who make up the Business Roundtable are replacing the organization's decades-old statement of purpose with a new one that looks at all stakeholders. The Business Roundtable's view since the 1970s has been that a company's guiding star should be maximizing value for shareholders. Today, the leading CEOs who make up this influential organization want companies to consider the interests of all stakeholders, their communities, and the country.

According to research from the Brookings Institution[5] that I mentioned earlier, Millennials make purchasing decisions based on the affinity they have with the values demonstrated by companies. This means that a company's financial success may well become more closely correlated with non-financial metrics.

Success for controllers will mean becoming more of a business partner to your organization. Automation and AI will largely take over our responsibilities for assembling information and reporting it. That gives us the time to be more of a copilot to the business. Controllers won't be just information gatherers and distributors, but as business partners, we'll be executing changes based on that data.

As Jerry Raphael, CFO of StackOverflow, puts it, "The controller is the drumbeat of the entire company. You set the cadence."

On the personal side, success may be more about achieving a better work-life balance, or perhaps more accurately, finding work that we care about deeply and which doesn't completely consume our lives. Success might not be measured by job title or the number of zeros in our paychecks, but in our personal and professional growth and the satisfaction we gain from doing our jobs well.

Success in our jobs also means creating a place where people enjoy coming to work, and where they feel supported professionally and personally. It means creating the team that everyone in the company wants to be on, which means that you've nailed culture.

CULTURE

As we've seen, a company's culture is vital for getting the best out of your team, and keeping the best players on your team in place. Culture will play an increasingly important role in the future. A positive workplace culture correlates with engagement and enables productive teams to form. Engaged employees on good teams stay around longer. Spending time and resources to develop a good culture is beginning to be seen less as a nice-to-have extra, and more as a must-have for attracting and keeping the best in a tight talent market.

Cultural fit will be more important in hiring decisions than scoring 100% on a scorecard of desirable skills. Skills can be taught, but cultural fit and being a team player, not so much. As Simon Sinek wrote in *Start with Why*,

> Great companies don't hire skilled people and motivate them, they hire already motivated people and inspire them. People are either motivated or they are not. Unless you give motivated people something to believe in, something bigger than their job to work toward, they will motivate themselves to find a new job and you'll be stuck with whoever's left.[6]

Whoever's left will likely be unmotivated, and may be more interested in putting in the time that they hope will get them to the next rung on the career ladder. But as I'll discuss below, that may not work out too well.

TEAMS AS THE BASIC WORK UNIT

Accounting departments in the future will look different than today. There will be fewer people, for one thing. The people who succeed in the future will be highly motivated and very interested in accounting, technical guidance, and, of course, technology.

With fewer people, working together as a team and leveraging tech will be essential. These smaller teams will be more efficient, and the members will need a much better knowledge set to stay relevant. This efficiency will come in part because the successful companies will always be implementing the technology that accountants need to stay one step ahead of the game.

Besides being on a smaller team, members of the accounting department will likely be on multiple cross-functional teams made up of people from across the organization. These teams will come together for specific projects rather than acting as siloed departments. Being on dynamic or cross-functional teams appears to make for more engaged workers, as a recent ADP Research Institute study confirmed.[7] They found that the most engaged workers were those on teams that were either dynamic or cross-departmental.

TEAMWORK REQUIRES MORE COLLABORATION

Collaboration will be more important than ever, and your team will need tech tools to keep in touch. Keep in mind that many of your team members may be remote for all or part of their work time. Remote leadership is different from on-site leadership. It takes more effort to keep everyone rowing in synchrony when they can't see each other, so using tools like Slack and Zoom to communicate will pick up some of the … slack. That's what we use here at FloQast.

Success in collaboration also requires trust and accountability, which is why FloQast has a built-in dashboard. This dashboard lets everyone see what tasks have been assigned to which person, and the progress of the close at a glance. Status meetings won't be necessary in the future.

Executives are already looking for a more collaborative culture, according to a recent survey by Bloomberg and CultureIQ.[8] They asked 300 senior executives what they thought the top cultural attributes of a high-performance workplace will be over the next three years. According to their findings, adaptive and agile (81%), collaborative (63%), engaged (48%), and innovative (47%) were the top features these executives will be looking for. Accountants who prefer to spend their days hiding behind that spreadsheet masterpiece will need to learn to work with others.

EMBRACE CHANGE TO REDUCE RISK

Accountants by nature tend to be conservative, and many who have spent time as auditors can have a tough time shaking the SALY mentality, so being adaptive and agile may pose a challenge. But as I discussed in the section on risk, embracing change can be a good way to decrease risk.

WHAT IS YOUR WHY?

Culture also means fine-tuning your company's and your department's **Why**. Communicating that clearly, and embodying that in everything you do will be more important than ever. Your **Why** shouldn't be just a nicely framed document, but part of the reason that everyone does the work they do. Embodying that Why in your approach to leading your team will really help them understand why they're doing what they're doing.

Don't be surprised if that leads to innovative and creative ideas for new products, or new ways of doing the work, or ways to help other parts of your organization, especially if those ideas come from a brand-new person or someone low in your organization. Here's where ego really needs to step out of the way. Who that person is and where that idea came from has got to be less important than seizing that idea and acting on it. Just make sure you give that person credit.

Every organization has brilliant people hidden in their organization. True leaders find those diamonds in the rough, and polish them.

TECHNOLOGY CAN HELP YOU CREATE A BETTER CULTURE

Throughout this book, I've spent a lot of time talking about how important people skills are. One common objection people have to tech is that it puts distance between people. It acts as a barrier and separates us. But as the authors of *The Future of the Professions* point out, using technology increases the opportunity for meaningful personal interactions, and helps "professionals to make more effective use of the limited time they have for any face-to-face exchange."[9] For example, in the medical field, the preponderance of online platforms such as WebMD means that patients can arrive at a doctor's appointment fairly well educated about their health and possible treatment options, so their limited time with the doctor may be more useful for both parties.

For controllers, tools like the dashboard and Review Notes in FloQast mean that conversations with team members can take place at a higher level. You're no longer asking **if** that task has been completed, but whether there's **a better way** to complete it. You're no longer nagging, but working with your team at a higher level.

Before you can use technology to create a better culture, you need a team and company culture that embraces technology. A team that's not just looking for linear improvements in processes, but one that's looking for the exponential changes that the tech of the future will bring us: a team that's looking ahead to what tomorrow's tech can do for your organization.

TECHNOLOGY

Accounting and finance touch every corner of an organization. But to have the greatest impact, we need tech as a partner. Tech makes the best partner when we take the time to figure out what problems we want it to solve, rather than just aimlessly buying the latest bells and whistles.

Implemented correctly, tech will free us from tasks that aren't adding value by giving us the bandwidth to support the business instead of just moving data around. Tech will give us insights to help our organizations reach their objectives. And tech will help us hire and retain the best and brightest.

No one can truly and honestly predict what the accounting tech of the future will be like. The best we can do is make educated guesses about the general trajectory of trends we see now. We can predict that there will be more of it, and that investments in accounting tech will be an important way to get the work done with a smaller workforce.

From Daniel Burrus' book *The Anticipatory Organization,* besides the three digital accelerators of exponentially increasing computing power, bandwidth, and digital storage, let's take a look at three hard trends that are relevant for controllers.

DATA ANALYTICS

The promise of data analytics is that we can gain insight into our company and our customers when we look at our numbers in new ways. Right now, just using existing analytical tools, here at FloQast, we can get an idea about what types of customers are likely to be the most profitable, and steer our sales teams towards those kinds of prospects.

Our Flux Analysis and Close Analytics are tools that make it easier to understand your data and your processes. Flux Analysis integrates with your ERP and allows you to add explanations that stay there, so you don't have to rely on finding the correct version of the right spreadsheet (and hoping that one has everyone's updates) to find what someone said months ago about a particular variance. Close Analytics lets you track in real time your progress toward the close, so you can keep a better handle on it.

In the future, data analytics tools combined with higher powered computing will be able to handle the massive data sets coming our way. As more of our world becomes interconnected with smart devices everywhere, we'll be inundated with data. We'll need tools and specialists to make sense of it all. That additional data and detailed analysis will mean that controllers will be able to provide more granular insights to the rest of our organizations. To do that, controllers will definitely have to be out of the weeds.

ARTIFICIAL INTELLIGENCE

We are at the very brink of what I think will be an explosion of AI in accounting tech. Our latest product, AutoRec, uses AI to reconcile hundreds of thousands of transactions in minutes, not days. Tech like this will keep you out of the debits and credits and operating at a higher level so you and your team can spend more time on the value-added tasks.

In the not-too-distant future, efficient accounting systems will have bots monitoring transactions for things that look odd. When something out of the ordinary pops up, your accounting manager, and maybe even your auditor, will get a text about it. With our current systems, suspicious transactions may not pop up until months later, if at all.

CLOUD

Not everyone is on the cloud yet, but we're moving that way. Besides being able to access your data and work from anywhere in the world, cloud tech means saying goodbye to integrating systems that weren't designed to work together. It means an end to painful upgrades to the next version of your ERP. Your IT department can focus on building things that make a difference, instead of trying to fix things that never work quite right. You'll never outgrow your servers because you can easily scale up and down as needed. And in today's world of constant cyber attacks, you have a more robust system to protect your data.

EMBRACE TECH AS A PARTNER

The combination of these three trends plus the ongoing exponential changes to computing power, bandwidth, and storage, mean that you always have to be embracing technology. You have to be looking ahead every year because something new will come out, and you have to be open to it. Maybe ignoring salespeople is not as good of an idea as it has been in the past because they're trying to bring good tools to you.

A DOWNSIDE TO AUTOMATION?

Automation frees us from the mind-numbing, tedious, non-value-added manual tasks that have consumed the lives of accountants and controllers for centuries. That freedom means that we get to do higher-level work that's way more interesting than trying to track down reconciling items among thousands of transactions.

But that also means we have to step up our game. Knowledge work is demanding. It means being at the top of your game every day. It means you have to take care of your body and your brain. There's no more sleep-walking through days of routine and repetitive tasks. No more taking a mental break by doing some really boring data entry.

Not everyone will thrive in such an intellectually demanding workplace. We will most likely need to restructure the expectations of the workplace so we have more downtime. We also need to create a culture at work where people feel supported when they need to take a break.

For those of us who thrive in a fast-paced and exciting environment, automation means less stress. It means more mental bandwidth to do the fun work, and a better work-life balance.

HOW DO WE GET THERE?

As I mentioned back in Chapter 5 (See Review Note: A new shape for your org chart), the finance team of the future will have a different shape, more like a diamond than a pyramid, with more people in the middle and fewer people at the bottom.

Today, as CEO of a tech company, that's what I'm building. If you look at our org chart on paper, it's still a pyramid. We've got staff engineers, senior engineers, and managers. But if you take a look at their skill set, and compare it to engineering departments from 15 years ago, ours would look like a diamond.

We don't have the bottom half of the pyramid because Cullen and our coding team aren't writing HTML code manually, line by line. Software engineers have created developer tools over the years that automate the tedious work so they can work at a higher level.

This diamond shape, with a fat middle layer of highly skilled people, is what the accounting team of the future will look like, and that's what I've built with engineers in a tech company.

The challenge here will be building that fat middle layer. When your bottom layer is the biggest, and it's made up of new college graduates and recent refugees from public accounting, like it is now in most accounting departments, then by natural selection and attrition, fewer and fewer make it up to the next level. Some that don't make it are a poor cultural fit, while others just aren't cut out to be higher-level accountants.

But as the bottom level gets smaller, that means you have fewer and fewer candidates with the knowledge and skills needed for the higher level work in the middle. How do you get people to have the experience they need to become one of those people in the middle?

Universities are far behind. Most accounting programs are tailored so that graduates can pass the CPA exam. That emphasis on tying the curriculum to the content of the CPA exam means that college coursework is years behind what accountants actually need to know today.

Since the CPA exam is administered at the state and territory level, the AICPA and NASBA have to work with 55 boards of accountancy to get changes approved. Depending on the state, that might mean new legislation before the content of the CPA exam can change. The changes to the exam that are relevant in year one may not show up on the exam until year five or later, which is when college courses will start reflecting those year one changes. Then the process starts all over again.

That lag in relevance means that the CPA may become less important for accountants in industry as time goes on.

The CMA, on the other hand, is a credential, not a license issued by a government. It's administered by one global organization, the Institute of Management Accountants. As one of my CPA friends, a retired CFO and controller, says, "they're in the trenches."

In 2018, the IMA surveyed finance pros around the world about what they want accountants to know. Their responses reflected a desire for increased tech skills, and those changes will show up on the exam starting in January 2020.[10] Two years may still be a long time in today's exponentially changing tech world, but it's much faster than the CPA exam changes.

MOVING FORWARD IN YOUR CAREER WON'T BE CLIMBING A LADDER

The real world isn't like college or even like the Big Four anymore. In the real world, as opposed to the Big Four, you're not promoted in this rigid structure just by virtue of time passing. To get those positions in the middle layer, you have to be really good at what you do.

Accountants will need to throw out their old way of looking at moving up in their career, which won't be up a ladder anymore. The younger generation has already abandoned that notion. When I started out, the usual progression was to audit for three years, then move to industry to be a senior accountant for a few years, then move up to accounting manager for a few more years, and then get the controller's job. Promotions could come just by the fact of waiting a few years, and doing your time in a position. Those days are gone. That's not how it works anymore.

The good news is that this actually presents a great opportunity for people who really care about their career and who are willing to take the effort to learn what they need to know. These people will be promoted faster than under the old way. But the caveat is that you have to be really good, and you have to be willing to keep on learning and keep improving yourself.

THE MOST IMPORTANT SKILL FOR THE FUTURE

In the face of disruption, those who survive and thrive are the ones who are able to adapt to the new reality. That's why lifetime learning will be the most important skill for the future, as Kevin Johnson describes in a recent article in Forbes.[11] Johnson writes:

> You can't go wrong cultivating a growth mindset and

embracing the idea that you'll have to learn *something*. It doesn't matter if you graduated from college last year or 10 years ago. Your ability and willingness to continually build new knowledge and skills could spell the difference between a continuous upward trajectory and a career plateau.

The need to embrace lifetime learning is reinforced by recent research by the Brookings Institution on the impact of automation and AI.[12] According to their detailed report, about 25% of US jobs will face serious risk of disappearing through automation, especially in occupations where the majority of tasks are routine and predictable. These are chiefly clerical and factory jobs. Another 36% of jobs will face a lesser degree of task automation, which means that fewer people will be needed to get the work done. Accounting and finance jobs fall firmly in this sector.

The jobs with the smallest risk of loss through automation fall into categories at either end of the wage spectrum. At the high end will be the jobs that require a high degree of creativity and education, which would include controllers and CFOs. At the other end will be low paying personal care and domestic service work which isn't easily automatable due to a high degree of variability and a need to communicate with others.

To mitigate this disruption, the authors recommend that workers "develop a constant learning mindset and use it to work both with machines, and in ways machines cannot. That means workers will need to take a new approach to learning and skills development."

Some people will figure this out on their own, and will develop their own ongoing professional development curriculum. One of my CPA friends studied cello as an undergrad. He told me that sitting in a room with his cello and the music taught him how to figure things out by himself. It taught him how to learn.

If lifelong learning is a skill, that implies you can get better at it, which is what an article by Ulrich Boser in the Harvard Business Review says.[13] Boser says:

> A growing body of research is making it clear that learners are made, not born. Through the deliberate use of practice and dedicated strategies to improve our ability to learn, we can all develop expertise faster and more effectively. In short, we can all get better at getting better.

My co-founder Cullen says there's a strong parallel in the developer community. Because languages are changing so quickly, there's an attitude that if you're over 45, your knowledge is irrelevant unless you've kept up. Here's a quote by user jdickey from a Reddit discussion forum on that topic: "I've shipped code in over 25 different languages so far; the year you stop learning new languages is the year your career takes a controlled flight into terrain."[14] Ending your quest to learn new things and to become a better professional can be fatal to your career.

THE UNIVERSITY OF THE WORKPLACE

But most people aren't as self-motivated as my musician friend, and they'll need an outside push to get going. That means that employers will have to step up to the bar to retrain and upskill their people. The Brookings Institution report on automation and AI cites studies confirming the value of training in the workplace: "Employer-led trainings can improve firm output, enhance workers' career prospects, and help companies fill emerging critical needs." There definitely is a positive ROI on training.

Out in the real world, Amazon recently announced it was spending $700 million to train a third of its 300,000 people.[15] Amazon sees the path of automation headed right their way. And they know that getting people into that fat middle layer will become even harder as time goes on, when every company out there is fighting over the people with mid-level skills. So Amazon is building its own candidate pool to fill those mid-level positions. Amazon isn't trying to turn order-pickers into software engineers. They're trying to move some of their people a few rungs up the career ladder.

Offering professional development will also help you hang on to those sometimes fickle Millennials, according to Deloitte's survey,[16] where they found that 73% of those planning to stay more than 5 years said their organization was a strong provider of training and education.

On the low-cost side, maybe you start leading education sessions once a month to start teaching the latest FASB standards. Maybe you're lucky and live somewhere where the state CPA society has great courses for corporate accountants. Or, as I mentioned in the section on people, you can help your team members put together a custom curriculum with resources from online training and outside instructors.

Here at FloQast, we've created a culture of learning. We put a cadence into it, so that it's not just something you do as an annual update, but as an ongoing part of being on the FloQast team. Each department does different things for their team members.

For the marketing team, we support SalesForce certification. We support continuing education for our CPAs. We get a budget for our engineers to attend Amazon's conference, so they can optimize their use of AWS. Engineering does a lot of things within their own organization to encourage learning, so they'll do brown bag training sessions where someone will give a presentation about the coolest new technology. Sales has group training sessions where they talk about what's been good and what went wrong, and they work together to get better at sales.

Another thing we do to support our people is to give them opportunities in different functional roles. For example, Troy Patipanavat started in customer success, then moved over to handle our social media. We have a handful of people who have done radically different things in the company. Some people are just so good and so versatile that they can work almost anywhere in the company, and they'll be great at anything they do. With those people, it's a matter of figuring out a spot where they can be most impactful for the business. And sometimes that changes over time.

DO YOU REALLY NEED A COLLEGE DEGREE TO BE AN ACCOUNTANT?

People used to go to school and take the CPA exam, and then they had to keep all this information memorized, and in their heads at work. But now, with the internet, you don't need to have all the guidance memorized, as long as you understand the framework and have Google.

However, college courses haven't adapted to that reality. They don't teach students how to think or how to apply that guidance to tricky situations in the real world. They also don't teach students much (if anything) about how to use accounting tech to do their work. Learning to use Excel really doesn't count as tech.

What will be important in the future is to start training people how to operate in the real world. I think accounting should be more of a trade school dynamic. Right now, I'm putting my money where my mouth is and I'm working on a project with a professor at a community college in the Bay Area. We're creating a curriculum for a certification program to help the tech companies who are having a tough time hiring entry level accountants.

Over two years, students in this program will learn the fundamentals of accounting, how to use Excel and QuickBooks Online, and (of course!) how to close the books with FloQast. At the end of the program, they'll have a certificate and they'll be qualified to work right away. They won't have to spend the extra time or money getting a four-year degree that forces them to learn art history before they can get to the skills that will help them earn a living.

In the development world, Cullen tells me that people are opting not to go to college at all. Instead, they go to coding bootcamps or incubators, and learn the basics. Then they get hired right away and start getting real world experience, which is where all the learning really happens anyways.

The downside to a vocational two-year track for accounting is that it will be harder to get a CPA or a CMA since you need at least a four-year college degree to sit for either. But that may not be so important in the future.

DEVELOP THE ACCOUNTANTS YOU WANT BY TEACHING THEM

Community colleges and many four-year universities are always looking for reliable adjunct professors to teach their accounting courses. You usually don't need any education credentials to teach intermediate or advanced accounting. You just need to demonstrate some command of the material — which is second nature for every controller I know.

Teaching college courses is a win-win all around. The students get to meet someone who's actually working as an accountant, and they'll benefit from your real world experience and insights. You get to meet the latest group of students coming through classes, and you can pick the cream of the crop to join your team.

GET OUT OF YOUR CUBE AND THINK OF YOURSELF AS A SERVICE PROVIDER

Moving into the future means you have to start thinking of your accounting department as a service firm or an agency within the company, rather than just as a cost center. Similar to an external service firm, the accounting department serves other parts of your organization by providing financial and business knowledge. The recipients of your services — the other departments and the executives and managers who need your expertise — are your clients.

As the controller and the leader of a service firm that provides accounting services to your organization, you have the choice of just being an order taker — someone who responds to requests — or an expert advisor — someone who digs deeper into those external requests, and answers the questions they didn't know they needed answers to. That extra effort of being an advisor is what will really help move your organization forward.

The way you get those insights is by getting out of your cube or office and building relationships so you can develop an understanding of the functional areas of your company. The best case scenario would be to actually work in different areas of your company to develop a feeling for how those parts operate. Having a deep understanding of how the parts of your company operate makes you more effective as a controller.

Unfortunately, most companies realistically can't have people floating from area to area and taking responsibility for areas where they maybe don't have the knowledge or training. So if your company can't support a rotation to different areas, then you need to be willing to raise your hand and be willing to work on some cross-functional initiative. Don't just sit back and wait for those opportunities to come to you, because they won't. It won't magically fall into your lap.

Instead, identify a pain point you have with a process that's broken. Maybe Salesforce doesn't connect to NetSuite. Then go to your boss and ask if you can work on this with the people over in sales. You have to take the initiative to seek out and complete projects like that. That's the new world of how you move forward in your career.

We do that at FloQast. Here's what my co-founder Chris Sluty, does:

> *So with my team, we've got our day-to-day work that we need to get done. We need to make sure our customers are using FloQast to the best of its abilities, so at the end of the year they're going to renew. That is baseline. That is what our job description says.*
>
> *But everybody on the team has another initiative that they're working on this quarter. So giving them that and having them present on those projects at the end of the quarter, the whole team is going to take a big step forward because collectively we're all working on something else.*

Building the accounting team of the future will require changing your perspective from the rearview mirror to the front windshield. You'll have to develop the leadership skills to lead an intensely collaborative and most likely remote team. Lifelong learning will be a must. You'll have to embrace change as a constant. You'll have to get comfortable with being uncomfortable. But for those who are willing to view their jobs as being the neutral center, the Switzerland of their organizations, being a Modern Controller will be the best job you'll ever have.

CONCLUSION

HANG ON FOR AN EXCITING RIDE

Having a vision for what you want is not enough. Vision without execution is hallucination.
–Thomas A. Edison

Over in the world of cryptocurrency investors, they use this acronym that looks like a spelling mistake: HODL: Hold On for Dear Life.

That's what the future will be like from now on. No matter

how fast you think the world is changing today, this is the slowest pace of change you'll see for the rest of your life. Myself, I can't wait to see the changes, and I'll rejoice when the really boring parts of what accountants do go away. And, hey, I'll even be happy if accounting tech advances to the point where no one needs a close management system because everything is already reconciled in real time.

Capitalizing on the coming changes means educating yourself about those changes, and being willing to take the risks that others are afraid to. It means throwing away the stereotype of an accountant as a boring and introverted bean counter, as just the compiler and reconciler of numbers, and stepping into your new role as leader of the information center of your organization.

It also means stepping up your leadership skills and being committed to becoming a better person, and helping everyone on your team get to their best potential. Building a great team will become one of your most important responsibilities.

The ones who get all of this right will have the best jobs in business. And they'll be part of the best companies on the planet.

Now go do that!

ACKNOWLEDGMENTS

When the idea of writing a book was floated by me I immediately accepted. I should have thought a little harder and tried to process just how much effort goes into writing a book.

I had a lot of help on this book and, as such, have many people to acknowledge.

I want to start by thanking the Accounting profession at large. When I started in 2006, I was already jaded about the job (and still am). But what I'm not jaded about is the people in the profession. Accountants are stereotyped as nerds, but that's a half-truth.

In founding FloQast I've been able to meet thousands of accountants and have drawn a different conclusion. Society rips on us, so we've created a survival mechanism — self deprecating humor. Because of this dynamic we've become comfortable in our own skin.

Accountants simply "keep it real" and that is a trait I admire greatly. I'm very proud to be part of the people in this industry. Everybody has a nerdy interest, it's just that accountants talk about it.

To Luca Pacioli for inventing double entry bookkeeping. Accrual accounting was the inspiration for FloQast, which ultimately led to this book. Without Luca none of this happens.

To our investors, employees, and customers because without you, none of this would have happened. You've supported our cause and helped FloQast put a dent in the accounting world.

To Blake Oliver, Wynn White and Troy Patipanavat for helping push the book to publication. Your efforts are greatly appreciated.

To Liz Farr, our Developmental Editor, who possesses a rare combination of wordsmithing, accounting expertise, and being a pleasure to work with. Thank you for all of your efforts, this book doesn't get done without you.

Finally, I'd like to thank my co-founders, Cullen Zandstra and Chris Sluty for joining me on this journey. It's been an unbelievable time and I'm so excited for the future of FloQast.

ABOUT THE AUTHOR

Mike Whitmire, CPA*, is CEO and Co-founder of FloQast, a provider of close management software created by accountants for accountants to help them close faster and more accurately. Prior to founding FloQast, Mike was part of the accounting and finance team at rapidly growing Cornerstone OnDemand. Helping prepare for their IPO, it was at the Los Angeles company where Mike came up with the idea that would become FloQast.

Mike began his career in audit at Ernst & Young, where his focus was on media and entertainment. During his time at EY, he performed public company audits, opening balance sheet audits, cash to GAAP restatements, compilation reviews, international reporting, merger and acquisition audits, and SOX compliance testing. Mike graduated from Syracuse University with a Bachelor's degree in Accounting.

*inactive

NOTES

INTRODUCTION

1. "Understanding the Modern Controller: A Survey of Financial Controllers," FloQast, February 2019, https://floqast.com/research/modern-controller-survey-findings/
2. "Volatility Report 2018", Crist|Kolder Associates, accessed December 18, 2018, http://www.cristkolder.com/volatility-report/
3. "The changing role of the financial controller," Ernst & Young, 2008. https://www.ey.com/Publication/vwLUAssets/Changing_role_of_the_financial_controller/$FILE/EY_Financial_controller_changing_role.pdf
4. "Stepping Outside the Box: Elevating the Role of the Controller," Deloitte, 2018. https://www2.deloitte.com/content/dam/Deloitte/us/Documents/risk/us-rfa-stepping-outside-box-elevating-role-controller.pdf
5. "Crunch Time I: Finance in a digital world," Deloitte. 2016 https://www2.deloitte.com/content/dam/Deloitte/us/Documents/finance-transformation/us-ft-crunch-time-finance-in-a-digital-world.pdf
6. Susskind, Richard and Daniel Susskind, *The Future of the Professions,* (New York: Oxford University Press, 2015), p. 110.
7. Jim Bell, "The Two-Step Process for Achieving Agility," CFO.com, March 7, 2019, http://www.cfo.com/operations/2019/03/the-two-step-process-for-achieving-agility/
8. "Finance 2020: Death by Digital," Accenture, 2015. https://www.accenture.com/t20150902T015110__w__/us-en/_acnmedia/Accenture/Conversion-Assets/DotCom/Documents/Global/PDF/Dualpub_21/Accenture-Finance-2020-PoV.pdf
9. "Will a robot take your job," *Technology (blog), BBC News,* September 11, 2015, https://www.bbc.com/news/technology-34066941
10. "The $8.5 Trilion Talent Shortage," *Reports & Insights, Korn Ferry Institute,* May 9, 2018, https://www.kornferry.com/institute/talent-crunch-future-of-work
11. "CFO Signals: What America's top finance executives are thinking — and doing" (full report), Deloitte, 4th quarter 2018, https://www2.deloitte.com/content/dam/Deloitte/us/Documents/finance/us-cfo-signals-4q18-full-report.pdf
12. "Reengineering Work: Don't Automate, Obliterate." Michael Hammer,

Harvard Business Review, July-August 1990. https://hbr.org/1990/07/reengineering-work-dont-automate-obliterate

2. A FRAMEWORK FOR THE MODERN CONTROLLER

1. Charles B. Eldridge and Kenneth R. Brousseau, Ph.D., "Navigating the Uncertain Road from CONTROLLER to CFO," *Executive Insight, Korn Ferry Institute*, February 7, 2007, https://www.kornferry.com/institute/197-navigating-the-uncertain-road-from-controller-to-cfo
2. "Volatility Report 2018", Crist|Kolder Associates, accessed December 18, 2018, http://www.cristkolder.com/volatility-report/
3. "State of the American Workplace,". Gallup, 2017. https://www.gallup.com/workplace/238085/state-american-workplace-report-2017.aspx
4. Ibid., p. 68.
5. "State of the American Workplace,". Gallup, 2017, p. 61. https://www.gallup.com/workplace/238085/state-american-workplace-report-2017.aspx
6. Jim Collins, *From Good to Great: Why Some Companies Make the Leap and Others Don't,"* (New York: HarperCollins Publishers Inc.), pg 41.
7. Simon Sinek, *Start with Why: How Great Leaders Inspire Everyone to Take Action*, (New York: Penguin Group (USA) Inc., 2009), p. 93.
8. "Understanding the Modern Controller: A Survey of Financial Controllers," FloQast, February 2019, https://floqast.com/research/modern-controller-survey-findings/
9. Susskind, Richard and Daniel Susskind, *The Future of the Professions*, (New York: Oxford University Press, 2015), p. 113.
10. "Data Never Sleeps 6.0," DOMO, 2018. https://web-assets.domo.com/blog/wp-content/uploads/2018/06/18_domo_data-never-sleeps-6verticals.pdf
11. "Finance 2025: Digital Transformation in Finance," Deloitte, 2016. https://www2.deloitte.com/content/dam/Deloitte/us/Documents/finance-transformation/us-ft-crunch-time-V-finance-2025.pdf
12. https://floqast.com/webinars/best-practices-month-end-close-oracle-netsuite-2/
13. "ERP Facts and Stats — and Lessons Learned," *TEC Blog Post, Technology Evaluation Centers*, June 5, 2018, https://www3.technologyevaluation.com/research/article/erp-software-facts-stats-and-lessons-learned.html.
14. "ERP Survey: The Real Facts About ERP Implementation," Mint Jutras, January 2019, https://ultraconsultants.com/erp-education/white-papers/erp-implementation-survey/.

3. WHY ARE PEOPLE SUCH A PROBLEM?

1. James Manyika et al., "Jobs Lost, Jobs Gained: Workforce Transitions in a Time of Automation," McKinsey Global Institute, December 2017. https://www.mckinsey.com/~/media/mckinsey/featured%20insights/

future%20of%20organizations/what%20the%20future%20of%20work%20will%20mean%20for%20jobs%20skills%20and%20wages/mgi%20jobs%20lost-jobs%20gained_report_december%202017.ashx
2. Jacques Bughin et al., "Skill Shift: Automation and the Future of the Workforce," McKinsey Global Institute, May 2018, https://www.mckinsey.com/~/media/McKinsey/Featured%20Insights/Future%20of%20Organizations/Skill%20shift%20Automation%20and%20the%20future%20of%20the%20workforce/MGI-Skill-Shift-Automation-and-future-of-the-workforce-May-2018.ashx
3. ""World Development Report 2019: The Changing Nature of Work," World Bank Group, 2019. http://www.worldbank.org/en/publication/wdr2019
4. Jacques Bughin et al., "Skill Shift: Automation and the Future of the Workforce," McKinsey Global Institute, May 2018, https://www.mckinsey.com/~/media/McKinsey/Featured%20Insights/Future%20of%20Organizations/Skill%20shift%20Automation%20and%20the%20future%20of%20the%20workforce/MGI-Skill-Shift-Automation-and-future-of-the-workforce-May-2018.ashx
5. "Future of Work: The Global Talent Crunch," Korn Ferry, May, 2018. https://www.kornferry.com/press/korn-ferry-study-reveals-global-talent-shortage-could-threaten-business-growth-around-the-world
6. Russell Heimlich, "Baby Boomers Retire," *Fact Tank: News in the Numbers (blog), Pew Research Center,* December 29, 2010. https://www.pewresearch.org/fact-tank/2010/12/29/baby-boomers-retire/
7. Mark Muro, Robert Maxim, and Jacob Whiton, "Automation and Artificial Intelligence: How machines are affecting people and places," Brookings Institution, January 2019, https://www.brookings.edu/research/automation-and-artificial-intelligence-how-machines-affect-people-and-places/

4. CULTURE IS THE KEY

1. Marcus Buckingham and Ashley Goodall, *Nine Lies About Work: A Free-thinking Leader's Guide to the Real World,* (Boston: Harvard Business Review Press. 2019), p. 24.
2. Ibid., p. 25.

5. MAKING PEOPLE YOUR MOST IMPORTANT ASSET

1. "How to Make the Accountant Unemployment Rate Work for You," *The Robert Half Blog,* October 10, 2019, https://www.roberthalf.com/blog/job-market/a-look-at-the-quarterly-accountant-unemployment-rate.
2. "The Demand for Skilled Talent," *Special Report,* Volume 17, Q1/Q2 2019, Robert Half, https://www.roberthalf.com/sites/default/files/documents/RH_Demand_Skilled_Talent_Vol17_US.pdf
3. Jeff Drew, "How to Win the Game of Talent," *Journal of Accountancy,*

October 1, 2015. https://www.journalofaccountancy.com/issues/2015/oct/cpa-firm-hiring-talent.html.
4. "Cloud Technology Advances the Accounting Profession," FloQast and Dimensional Research, June 2018, https://floqast.com/research/cloud-technology-advances-the-accounting-profession-a-survey-of-accounting-and-finance-professionals/.
5. Susan M. Heathfield, "Why Generational Differences are a Workplace Myth," *Human Resources: Culture (blog), The Balance*, October 8, 2018, https://www.thebalancecareers.com/do-not-focus-on-workplace-generational-differences-4153271.
6. Morley Winograd and Dr. Michael Hais, "How Millennials Could Upend Wall Street and Corporate America,", *Governance Studies at Brookings,* May, 2014, https://www.brookings.edu/wp-content/uploads/2016/06/Brookings_Winogradfinal.pdf.
7. Morley Winograd and Dr. Michael Hais, "How Millennials Could Upend Wall Street and Corporate America,", *Governance Studies at Brookings,* May, 2014, https://www.brookings.edu/wp-content/uploads/2016/06/Brookings_Winogradfinal.pdf.
8. "2018 Deloitte Millennial Survey," Deloitte, January 22, 2018, https://www2.deloitte.com/content/dam/Deloitte/global/Documents/About-Deloitte/gx-2018-millennial-survey-report.pdf.
9. Andie Burjek, "Baby Boomers Booming as Gig Workers," *Benefits (blog), Workforce,* February 20, 2018, https://www.workforce.com/2018/02/20/baby-boomers-booming-gig-workers/.
10. "2018 Deloitte Millennial Survey," Deloitte, January 22, 2018, https://www2.deloitte.com/content/dam/Deloitte/global/Documents/About-Deloitte/gx-2018-millennial-survey-report.pdf.
11. Jim Collins, *From Good to Great: Why Some Companies Make the Leap and Others Don't,"* (New York: HarperCollins Publishers Inc.), pg 42.
12. Ibid., pg 50.
13. "Cloud Technology Advances the Accounting Profession," FloQast and Dimensional Research, June 2018, https://floqast.com/research/cloud-technology-advances-the-accounting-profession-a-survey-of-accounting-and-finance-professionals/
14. Data Analytics Certificate Program, AICPA, https://certificates.aicpastore.com/certificates/data-analytics
15. https://www.udemy.com/courses/search/?src=ukw&q=data+analytics
16. Ann Marie Maloney, "Top Google exec says accountants can be creative - here's how,"*News (blog), Association of International Certified Professional Accountants,* September 25, 2018, https://www.aicpa-cima.com/news/top-google-exec-says-accountants-can-be-creative-too.html.
17. "Creative Problem Solving," Creative Education Foundation, http://www.creativeeducationfoundation.org/creative-problem-solving/.
18. Leigh Kunis, "Data Analyst vs. Data Scientist," *Springboard blog,* December 17, 2018. https://www.springboard.com/blog/data-analyst-vs-data-sc
19. Jonny Brooks-Bartlett, "Here's why so many data scientists are leaving their jobs," *Towards Data Science (blog),* March 28, 2018, https://

towardsdatascience.com/why-so-many-data-scientists-are-leaving-their-jobs-a1f0329d7ea4.

20. Monica Rogati, "The AI Hierarchy of Needs," *Hackernoon*, June 12, 2017, https://hackernoon.com/the-ai-hierarchy-of-needs-18f111fcc007.
21. "2018 Deloitte Millennial Survey," Deloitte, January 22, 2018, https://www2.deloitte.com/content/dam/Deloitte/global/Documents/About-Deloitte/gx-2018-millennial-survey-report.pdf.
22. Liz Farr, CPA, "How organizations can streamline the month-end close," *Journal of Accountancy*, March 1, 2018, https://www.journalofaccountancy.com/issues/2018/mar/streamline-month-end-close.html.
23. Geoff Smart, *Who: The A Method for Hiring*, (New York: Random House Inc., 2008).
24. "2018 Deloitte Millennial Survey," Deloitte, January 22, 2018, https://www2.deloitte.com/content/dam/Deloitte/global/Documents/About-Deloitte/gx-2018-millennial-survey-report.pdf.
25. "State of the American Workplace,". Gallup, 2017. https://www.gallup.com/workplace/238085/state-american-workplace-report-2017.aspx, pg. 69.
26. "2018 Deloitte Millennial Survey," Deloitte, January 22, 2018, https://www2.deloitte.com/content/dam/Deloitte/global/Documents/About-Deloitte/gx-2018-millennial-survey-report.pdf.
27. "Agile Finance Unleashed: The Key Traits of Digital Finance Leaders" AICPA and CIMA, January 17, 2019, https://www.cgma.org/content/dam/cgma/resources/reports/downloadabledocuments/agile-finance-unleashed-aicpa-cima-oracle.pdf
28. Lauren Weber, "Why Companies are Failing at Reskilling," *Wall Street Journal*, April 19, 2019. https://www.wsj.com/articles/the-answer-to-your-companys-hiring-problem-might-be-right-under-your-nose-11555689542.
29. Jacques Bughin et al., "Skill Shift: Automation and the Future of the Workforce," McKinsey Global Institute, May 2018, https://www.mckinsey.com/~/media/McKinsey/Featured%20Insights/Future%20of%20Organizations/Skill%20shift%20Automation%20and%20the%20future%20of%20the%20workforce/MGI-Skill-Shift-Automation-and-future-of-the-workforce-May-2018.ashx
30. Lauren Weber, " The 'Hybrid' Skills that Tomorrow's Jobs Will Require," *Wall Street Journal*, January 22, 2019, https://www.wsj.com/articles/the-hybrid-skills-that-tomorrows-jobs-will-require-1154799426.
31. "Hybrid Jobs: What Are They (And How Can You Get One)?" *The Robert Half Blog*, December 1, 2016, https://www.roberthalf.com/blog/job-market/hybrid-jobs-what-are-they-and-how-can-you-get-one.
32. Thomas W. Malone, "What AI Will Do to Corporate Hierarchies," *Wall Street Journal*, April 1, 2019, https://www.wsj.com/articles/what-ai-will-do-to-corporate-hierarchies-11554158120?mod=searchresults&page=1&pos=1.
33. "The Changing Shape of the Finance Function," CGMA, June 2, 2018, https://www.cgma.org/resources/reports/changing-shape-of-the-finance-function.html.
34. Mark Muro, Robert Maxim, and Jacob Whiton, "Automation and Artifi-

cial Intelligence: How machines are affecting people and places," Brookings Institution, January 2019, https://www.brookings.edu/research/automation-and-artificial-intelligence-how-machines-affect-people-and-places/

6. TRUST IS THE GLUE THAT BUILDS TEAMS

1. "State of the American Workplace,". Gallup, 2017. https://www.gallup.com/workplace/238085/state-american-workplace-report-2017.aspx, p. 116.
2. Paul J. Zak, "The Neuroscience of Trust," *Harvard Business Review*, January-February 2017. https://hbr.org/2017/01/the-neuroscience-of-trust.
3. "2014 Work and Well-Being Survey," American Psychological Association, 2014, http://www.apaexcellence.org/assets/general/2014-work-and-wellbeing-survey-results.pdf?_ga=2.73937489.213297320.1566591958-1136466187.1566591958.
4. Marcus Buckingham and Ashley Goodall, *Nine Lies About Work: A Free-thinking Leader's Guide to the Real World*, (Boston: Harvard Business Review Press, 2019), p. 241.

7. ACCOUNTABILITY ISN'T JUST COMPLIANCE

1. "Accountability: The Low-Hanging Fruit for Optimizing Individual and Organizational Performance." Partners in Leadership, 2014. https://info.partnersinleadership.com/workplace-accountability-study-executive-summary-download
2. Randy Pennington, "Building a Culture of Accountability," *HR Magazine, The Society for Human Resource Management*, September 1, 2015, https://www.shrm.org/hr-today/news/hr-magazine/pages/0915-building-an-accountable-culture.aspx.
3. Matt Egan, "Wells Fargo uncovers up to 1.4 million more bank accounts," *CNN Business*, August 31, 2017, https://money.cnn.com/2017/08/31/investing/wells-fargo-fake-accounts/index.html.
4. Marcus Buckingham and Ashley Goodall, *Nine Lies About Work: A Free-thinking Leader's Guide to the Real World*, (Boston: Harvard Business Review Press, 2019), p. 142.
5. Marcus Buckingham and Ashley Goodall, "Reinventing Performance Management," *Harvard Business Review*, April 2015. https://hbr.org/2015/04/reinventing-performance-management.

8. CHALLENGES WITH RISK

1. Jayson Derrick, "Remember When Yahoo Turned Down $1 Million to Buy Google?" *Yahoo Finance (blog)*, July 25, 2016, https://finance.yahoo.com/news/remember-yahoo-turned-down-1-132805083.html. https://

finance.yahoo.com/news/remember-yahoo-turned-down-1-132805083.html

2. MG Siegler, "When Google Wanted To Sell To Excite For Under $1 Million — And They Passed," *TechCrunch*, September 29, 2010, https://techcrunch.com/2010/09/29/google-excite/.
3. Parmy Olsen, "Blackberry's Famous Last Words at 2007 iPhone Launch," *Forbes*, May 26, 2015, https://www.forbes.com/sites/parmyolson/2015/05/26/blackberry-iphone-book/#85eac3163c94.
4. "Cloud Technology Advances the Accounting Profession," FloQast and Dimensional Research, June 2018, https://floqast.com/research/cloud-technology-advances-the-accounting-profession-a-survey-of-accounting-and-finance-professionals/
5. Tatyana Shumsky, "Corporate Controllers Step into the Spotlight as CFO Role Evolves," *Wall Street Journal*, February 20. 2019, https://www.wsj.com/articles/corporate-controllers-step-into-the-spotlight-as-cfo-role-evolves-11550.682000.
6. "Cloud Technology Advances the Accounting Profession," FloQast and Dimensional Research, June 2018, https://floqast.com/research/cloud-technology-advances-the-accounting-profession-a-survey-of-accounting-and-finance-professionals/
7. "Stepping Outside the Box: Elevating the Role of the Controller," Deloitte, 2018. https://www2.deloitte.com/content/dam/Deloitte/us/Documents/risk/us-rfa-stepping-outside-box-elevating-role-controller.pdf
8. "From controller to strategic partner: A growing imperative," *Dbriefs Webcast (on demand)*, Deloitte, October 18, 2018, https://www2.deloitte.com/us/en/pages/dbriefs-webcasts/events/october/2018/dbriefs-from-controller-to-strategic-partner-growing-imperative.html.
9. "Cloud Technology Advances the Accounting Profession," FloQast and Dimensional Research, June 2018, https://floqast.com/research/cloud-technology-advances-the-accounting-profession-a-survey-of-accounting-and-finance-professionals/
10. "The changing role of the financial controller," Ernst & Young, 2008, https://www.ey.com/Publication/vwLUAssets/Changing_role_of_the_financial_controller/$FILE/EY_Financial_controller_changing_role.pdf .
11. Jessica Campisi and Samira Said, "America has just one Blockbuster left," CNN, July 13, 2018, https://www.cnn.com/2018/07/13/us/last-blockbuster-america-trnd/index.html.
12. Mark Beasley et al., "Executive Perspectives on Top Risks 2019," Protiviti and North Carolina State Enterprise Risk Management Initiative, 2019, https://www.protiviti.com/US-en/insights/protiviti-top-risks-survey.
13. Mark S. Beasley, Bruce C. Branson, and Bonnie V. Hancock, "2019 The State of Risk Oversight: An Overview of Enterprise Risk Management Practices," AICPA and North Carolina State Enterprise Risk Management Initiative, 2019, https://www.aicpa.org/content/dam/aicpa/interestareas/businessindustryandgovernment/resources/erm/downloadabledocuments/aicpa-erm-research-study-2019.pdf.

9. IMPLEMENT ALL THE TECH YOU CAN

1. "Mobile share of organic search engine visits in the United States from 3rd quarter 2013 to 2nd quarter 2019," Statista, 2019, https://www.statista.com/statistics/297137/mobile-share-of-us-organic-search-engine-visits/.
2. Drake Baer, "Google's genius futurist uses this zany Asian folktale to explain how technology will rule the future," *Business Insider*, July 30, 2015, https://www.businessinsider.com/ray-kurzweil-chinese-chess-folktale-2015-6.
3. Tibi Puiu, "Your smartphone is millions of times more powerful than all of NASA's combined computing in 1969," *News (blog), ZME, Science*, October 13, 2015, https://www.zmescience.com/research/technology/smartphone-power-compared-to-apollo-432/.
4. Greg Ip, "If the Economy Booms, Thank Software," *Wall Street Journal*, May 29, 2019, https://www.wsj.com/articles/if-the-economy-booms-thank-software-11559140991.
5. Jacques Bughin et al., "Skill Shift: Automation and the Future of the Workforce," McKinsey Global Institute, May 2018, pg 38, https://www.mckinsey.com/~/media/McKinsey/Featured%20Insights/Future%20of%20Organizations/Skill%20shift%20Automation%20and%20the%20future%20of%20the%20workforce/MGI-Skill-Shift-Automation-and-future-of-the-workforce-May-2018.ashx.
6. Ibid., pg 44.
7. Perry D. Wiggins, CPA, "Metric of the Month: Finance FTEs per $1B in Revenue," CFO.com, January 8, 2019, http://www.cfo.com/hiring/2019/01/metric-of-the-month-finance-ftes-per-1b-in-revenue/.
8. "The Connected Workforce: Maximizing Productivity, Creativity and Profitability," Harvard Business Revew Analytic Services, 2018, https://www.insight.com/en_US/learn/content/gated/hbr-the-connected-workforce-report-ac1147.html?utm_medium=pr&utm_source=GlobeNewswire&utm_campaign=Insight_HBR_ConnectedWorkforceStudy_NewsRelease.
9. "Cloud Technology Advances the Accounting Profession," FloQast and Dimensional Research, June 2018, https://floqast.com/research/cloud-technology-advances-the-accounting-profession-a-survey-of-accounting-and-finance-professionals/.
10. "Agile Finance Unleashed: The Key Traits of Digital Finance Leaders" AICPA and CIMA, January 17, 2019, https://www.cgma.org/content/dam/cgma/resources/reports/downloadabledocuments/agile-finance-unleashed-aicpa-cima-oracle.pdf.

10. FIX YOUR PROCESSES

1. "The Chaos of Month-End Close," FloQast, January 2017, https://floqast.com/research/the-chaos-of-month-end-close-a-survey-of-accounting-professionals/.

2. Frank Plaschke, Ishaan Seth, and Rob Whiteman, "Bots, Algorithms, and the Future of Finance," *Strategy & Corporate Finance - Our Insights (blog)*, McKinsey and Company, January 2018. https://www.mckinsey.com/business-functions/strategy-and-corporate-finance/our-insights/bots-algorithms-and-the-future-of-the-finance-function.

11. WHAT'S IN YOUR TOOLBOX?

1. "Agile Finance Unleashed: The Key Traits of Digital Finance Leaders" AICPA and CIMA, January 17, 2019, https://www.cgma.org/content/dam/cgma/resources/reports/downloadabledocuments/agile-finance-unleashed-aicpa-cima-oracle.pdf.
2. "2019 CFO Survey Report: All Systems Go: CFOs lead the way to a digital world," Grant Thornton, 2019, https://www.grantthornton.com/Insights/CFO-survey-2019.aspx.
3. Tatyana Shumsky, "Stop Using Excel, Finance Chiefs Tell Staffs," *Wall Street Journal*, November 29, 2017, https://www.wsj.com/articles/stop-using-excel-finance-chiefs-tell-staffs-1511346601?mod=article_inline.
4. Tim Worstall, "Microsoft's Excel Might Be the Most Dangerous Software on the Planet," Forbes, February 13, 2013, https://www.forbes.com/sites/timworstall/2013/02/13/microsofts-excel-might-be-the-most-dangerous-software-on-the-planet/#1f065601633d.
5. James Manyika et al., "Harnessing automation for a future that works," McKinsey Global Institute, January 2017, https://www.mckinsey.com/featured-insights/digital-disruption/harnessing-automation-for-a-future-that-works.
6. "Data is beautiful: 10 of the best data visualization examples from history to today," *Learning (blog)*, Tableau, https://www.tableau.com/learn/articles/best-beautiful-data-visualization-examples.
7. "2019 CFO Survey Report: All Systems Go: CFOs lead the way to a digital world," Grant Thornton, 2019, https://www.grantthornton.com/Insights/CFO-survey-2019.aspx.
8. Jim Dwyer and Emma Fitzsimmons, "$461,646 in Pay for One Worker: M.T.A. Overtime Scrutinized by Prosecutors," *New York Times*, May 17, 2019, https://www.nytimes.com/2019/05/17/nyregion/mta-overtime.html.

12. KNOWLEDGE CONNECTS EVERYTHING

1. G.C. Kane, et al., "Achieving Digital Maturity" *MIT Sloan Management Review* and Deloitte University Press, July 2017, https://www2.deloitte.com/au/en/pages/media-releases/articles/risk-averse-companies-struggle-digital-transformation-140717.html.
2. Richard Hilton, "CFOs must implore their business to use real-time data for accurate forecasting," ITProPortal, May 27, 2019, https://www.

itproportal.com/features/cfos-must-implore-their-business-to-use-real-time-data-for-accurate-forecasting/.

3. Jim Bell, "The Two Step Process for Achieving Agility," CFO.com, March 7, 2019, http://www.cfo.com/operations/2019/03/the-two-step-process-for-achieving-agility/.
4. "Cloud Technology Advances the Accounting Profession," FloQast and Dimensional Research, June 2018, https://floqast.com/research/cloud-technology-advances-the-accounting-profession-a-survey-of-accounting-and-finance-professionals/.
5. "The Connected Workforce: Maximizing Productivity, Creativity and Profitability," Harvard Business Review Analytic Services, 2018, https://www.insight.com/en_US/learn/content/gated/hbr-the-connected-workforce-report-ac1147.html?utm_medium=pr&utm_source=GlobeNewswire&utm_campaign=Insight_HBR_ConnectedWorkforceStudy_NewsRelease.
6. G.C. Kane, et al., "Achieving Digital Maturity" *MIT Sloan Management Review* and Deloitte University Press, July 2017, https://www2.deloitte.com/au/en/pages/media-releases/articles/risk-averse-companies-struggle-digital-transformation-140717.html.
7. Baruch Lev and Feng Gu, *The End of Accounting,* (Hoboken, NJ: John Wiley & Sons, Inc., 2016), pg 30.
8. Ibid., pg. 44.
9. Ibid., pg. 75.
10. Ronald J. Baker, *Measure What Matters to Customers: Using Key Predictive Indicators,* (Hoboken: John Wiley & Sons, Inc., 2006), p. 71.
11. "Agile Finance Unleashed: The Key Traits of Digital Finance Leaders" AICPA and CIMA, January 17, 2019, https://www.cgma.org/content/dam/cgma/resources/reports/downloadabledocuments/agile-finance-unleashed-aicpa-cima-oracle.pdf.
12. "Stepping Outside the Box: Elevating the Role of the Controller," Deloitte, 2018. https://www2.deloitte.com/content/dam/Deloitte/us/Documents/risk/us-rfa-stepping-outside-box-elevating-role-controller.pdf.
13. "Crunch time 7: Reporting in a digital world," Deloitte, 2018, https://www2.deloitte.com/content/dam/Deloitte/us/Documents/finance-transformation/us-crunch-time-seven-reporting-in-a-digital-world.pdf .
14. Ibid.
15. "Baruch Lev On the End of Accounting — Q&A," *Knowledge Leaders Capital Blog,* ValueWalk, September 16, 2016, https://www.valuewalk.com/2016/09/baruch-lev-end-accounting-qa/.
16. Baruch Lev and Feng Gu, *The End of Accounting,* (Hoboken, NJ: John Wiley & Sons, Inc., 2016), p. 126.
17. Tien Tzuo (with Gabe Weisert), *Subscribed: Why the Subscription Model Will Be Your Company's Future — and What to Do About It,* (New York, NY: Portfolio/Penguin, 2018), p. 178.
18. "2019 CFO Survey Report: All Systems Go: CFOs lead the way to a

digital world," Grant Thornton, 2019, https://www.grantthornton.com/Insights/CFO-survey-2019.aspx.

19. David McCann, "Amid Data Deluge, Judgment Still Makes the Difference," CFO.com, June 6, 2019, https://www.cfo.com/analytics/2019/06/amid-data-deluge-judgment-still-makes-the-difference/
20. G.C. Kane, et al., "Achieving Digital Maturity" *MIT Sloan Management Review* and Deloitte University Press, July 2017, https://www2.deloitte.com/au/en/pages/media-releases/articles/risk-averse-companies-struggle-digital-transformation-140717.html.
21. "The Connected Workforce: Maximizing Productivity, Creativity and Profitability," Harvard Business Review Analytic Services, 2018, https://www.insight.com/en_US/learn/content/gated/hbr-the-connected-workforce-report-ac1147.html?utm_medium=pr&utm_source=GlobeNewswire&utm_campaign=Insight_HBR_ConnectedWorkforceStudy_NewsRelease.
22. G.C. Kane, et al., "Achieving Digital Maturity" *MIT Sloan Management Review* and Deloitte University Press, July 2017, https://www2.deloitte.com/au/en/pages/media-releases/articles/risk-averse-companies-struggle-digital-transformation-140717.html.

13. CREATING THE ACCOUNTING TEAM OF THE FUTURE

1. Susskind, Richard and Daniel Susskind, *The Future of the Professions*, (New York: Oxford University Press, 2015), p. 155.
2. "Baruch Lev On the End of Accounting — Q&A," *Knowledge Leaders Capital Blog*, ValueWalk, September 16, 2016, https://www.valuewalk.com/2016/09/baruch-lev-end-accounting-qa/.
3. Cydney Posner, "What Happened at the Corp Fin Roundtable on Short-Termism?" Harvard Law School Forum on Corporate Governance and Financial Regulation, July 24, 2019, https://corpgov.law.harvard.edu/2019/07/24/what-happened-at-the-corp-fin-roundtable-on-short-termism/.
4. David Benoit, "Move Over Shareholders: Top CEOs Say Companies Have Obligations to Society," *Wall Street Journal*, August 19, 2019, https://www.wsj.com/articles/business-roundtable-steps-back-from-milton-friedman-theory-11566205200.
5. Morley Winograd and Dr. Michael Hais, "How Millennials Could Upend Wall Street and Corporate America,", *Governance Studies at Brookings*, May, 2014, https://www.brookings.edu/wp-content/uploads/2016/06/Brookings_Winogradfinal.pdf.
6. Simon Sinek, *Start with Why: How Great Leaders Inspire Everyone to Take Action*, (New York: Penguin Group (USA) Inc., 2009), p. 94.
7. Dr. Mary Hayes, Dr. Fran Chumney, Dr. Corinne Wright, Marcus Buckingham, "The Global Study of Engagement - Technical Report," ADP Research Institute, 2019, https://www.adp.com/resources/articles-and-insights/articles/g/global-study-of-engagement-technical-report.aspx?referrer={95522E03-C5DD-4626-8BE8-7D223D961259.

8. "The Future of Work: Strategy, Culture and HR's Role," CultureIQ and Bloomberg, HR Exchange Network, February, 2019, https://www.hrexchangenetwork.com/hr-tech/whitepapers/the-future-of-work-strategy-culture-and-hrs-role
9. Susskind, Richard and Daniel Susskind, *The Future of the Professions,* (New York: Oxford University Press, 2015), pg 249.
10. Michael Cohn, "IMA plans to update CMA exam with more of a tech focus," *Accounting Today,* January 3, 2019, https://www.accountingtoday.com/news/ima-plans-to-update-cma-exam-with-more-of-a-technology-focus.
11. Kevin H. Johnson, "The Most Important Skill for 21st Century Success," *Forbes,* July 31, 2018, https://www.forbes.com/sites/kevinhjohnson/2018/07/31/the-most-important-skill-for-21st-century-success/#c3c548232c88.
12. Mark Muro, Robert Maxim, and Jacob Whiton, "Automation and Artificial Intelligence: How machines are affecting people and places," Brookings Institution, January 2019, https://www.brookings.edu/research/automation-and-artificial-intelligence-how-machines-affect-people-and-places/
13. Ulrich Boser, "Learning is a Learned Behavior. Here's How to Get Better at It," *Harvard Business Review,* May 2, 2018, https://hbr.org/2018/05/learning-is-a-learned-behavior-heres-how-to-get-better-at-it.
14. "Web developers who are 45 and older? How is being a developer at that age in your career?" https://www.reddit.com/r/webdev/comments/3p4del/web_developers_who_are_45_and_older_how_is_being/
15. Ben Casselman and Adam Satariano, "Amazon's Latest Experiment: Retraining its Workforce," *New York Times,* July 19, 2018, https://www.nytimes.com/2019/07/11/technology/amazon-workers-retraining-automation.html.
16. "2018 Deloitte Millennial Survey," Deloitte, January 22, 2018, https://www2.deloitte.com/content/dam/Deloitte/global/Documents/About-Deloitte/gx-2018-millennial-survey-report.pdf.